BILL

PIONEER BUSH PILOT AND OUTFITTER

BENNETT

BILL

PIONEER BUSH PILOT AND OUTFITTER

BENNETT

A Biography by Len Rich

BREAKWATER BOOKS LTD.
JESPERSON PUBLISHING • BREAKWATER DISTRIBUTORS
www.breakwaterbooks.com

Library and Archives Canada Cataloguing in Publication

Rich, Len, 1938-
   Bill Bennett : pioneer bush pilot and outfitter : a biography / by Len Rich.

ISBN 978-1-55081-250-3

1. Bennett, Bill, 1931-2001.   2. Bush pilots--Newfoundland and Labrador--Biography.   3. Outfitters (Outdoor recreation)--Newfoundland and Labrador--Labrador--Biography. 4. Newfoundland and Labrador--Biography. I. Title.

TL540.B45R52 2008   629.13092   C2008-906625-1

The Canada Council | Le Conseil des Arts
for the Arts | du Canada

We acknowledge the financial support of The Canada Council for the Arts for our publishing activities.

We acknowledge the support of the Department of Tourism, Culture and Recreation for our publishing activities.

Canadä

We acknowledge the financial support of the Government of Canada through the Book Publishing Industry Development Program (BPIDP) for our publishing activities.

Printed in Canada

FOREWORD

Bill Bennett was an adventurer. We had a great relationship through the years, and he added a lot to my enjoyment of fishing in Labrador. I booked his places over several seasons and we always had good times with Bill at Wulff Lake, Sandhill and Michael's River.

Bill and I and our late friend Craig Dobbin shared some of the most fun experiences that I can recall. I don't know how much Bill gave me over the years, wading sticks and chairs and all sorts of other things, but it's quite a collection.

He built the finest lodges to be found in Labrador, and at some of the best locations to be found. The lodge at Michael's River is one of the most scenic places in Labrador, and I should know – I've flown over almost every inch of ground up there over the years. Bill Bennett was one of a kind. He'll never be replaced.

Harry Steele
Newfoundland businessman and friend

INTRODUCTION

I'LL ALWAYS REMEMBER when I received the call from Cathy Mitchinson, Bill's oldest daughter, asking if I would be interested in writing a book about her dad's life. "It would be an honour," I told her, and I meant it. He was a friend, one I had flown many miles with, and a mentor when it came to beginning my own outfitting business.

Bill Bennett had a full life, doing things he wanted to do, during a time when the province of Newfoundland and Labrador was in its infancy, just beginning its modern growth and joining the remainder of Canada as a result of Confederation. There were few roads in those days. Transportation links were primarily by coastal boat and river boat to reach the remote settlements which were built along the coastlines or on the banks and at mouths of rivers where there was abundant fresh water. Communities were severely isolated. Many families grew up and lived their entire lives without venturing farther than a few kilometers away from their homes on land. The sea was their livelihood. The only other option for transportation was aircraft, more specifically the bush planes. This is where Bill came into his own element.

Other than the city of St. John's, the paper towns of Grand Falls and Corner Brook, or the military bases at Argentia, Stephenville, or Goose Bay, there was no urban lifestyle to speak of. Perhaps that's why Bill, as a young lad, became so enamoured with the desire to become a pilot and to fly his own aircraft, to taste the freedom of flight.

From humble beginnings as a child in St. John's, he grew to be known as a keen businessman, a conservationist, a successful hunting and fishing outfitter, but most of all as an aviator with a passion for flying. During his lifetime he associated with some of the most powerful and some of the least powerful people of the province, but he treated them all alike.

So how does the world remember someone who has passed through and touched so many lives along the way? This is a question I asked myself over and over again as I began to write this biography. From the numbers of men and women from all walks of life who attended his funeral, it was obvious he was held in high esteem. Bill garnered a great deal of respect.

It took months of research and discussions with those who knew him best, his sister and his offspring and the people he worked with, those who worked for him, and the pilots who shared the same passion for flying, to learn more about the inner man. Unfortunately, many of the people he worked with or those who knew him better than others had also passed away during the interim. An era, a time, a generation of men and women who had been touched by Bill at some time in their lives were no longer here to recall those important memories. Many blank spaces remain in the story of Bill Bennett.

I was fortunate to have shared some of Bill's time during the final years of his life, and my thoughts are here as well. I knew Bill in a different way than the others, and each of us, I discovered, had varying impressions of him.

It is this composite of Bill Bennett that I have attempted to capture within these pages, a picture of a man who loved family, flying, and life. He made a lasting impression on all who met him or knew him.

He was a man who garnered respect. I hope this book does him justice.

PART ONE
THE EARLY YEARS

WILLIAM JAMES BENNETT entered the world on February 6, 1931, in the city of St. John's to parents Louise and Bill Bennett. He was the youngest child in the family. One sister, Dorothy, was the eldest, and a brother, Michael, was next in line. All three had been born within a three-year span. In those early days many children were born at home rather than a hospital, and midwives were more common than physicians in assisting with the births of children.

His father William, Sr., was in the military and away from home a great deal, so the task of raising the three children was left with their grandparents, Martha and Mike Bennett.

The years of Bill's youth are difficult to research. His older brother Michael passed away a few years following Bill's death in 2001, but his sister Dorothy was still living and could provide some memories of his young years.

Dorothy, 79 in 2007, recalled Bill as being very active as a young boy.

"Bill was a go-getter," she said. "He used to work for the telegraph office, delivering telegrams all over St. John's by bicycle. He took such good care of that bike; he would bring it into the front porch of the house every night and clean it up so it would look good the next day.

"He was always a good student and was going to the Catholic boys' school on Patrick Street. He never got into any trouble that I can remember.

"My uncle, Jimmy King, was rather well-to-do in those days; he took Bill under his wing when he was older and brought him to Gander. That was just after World War II, so he would have been about sixteen or seventeen then. He went to work with Trans Canada Airlines doing all sorts of things like cleaning the planes and loading baggage, so I guess that's where the flying bug got into his blood."

FRED SMEATON

A long-time friend and former employee, Fred Smeaton was 85 years young at the time of this writing, but his memory of those early years was still fairly intact.

"I first met Bill back in 1948. He was a baggage handler at the time, working at the air terminal for Frank Lawlor. My wife and Bill's wife Mary shared the same room and that's how we first came to know each other. I left in 1951 and went to St. John's to work for Hickman Motors and worked there for four years. I was an auto mechanic back then.

"There weren't many roads to drive on once you got out of St. John's, but eventually there was a road put through from Gander over to Glenwood, and Bill met a fellow from Corner Brook who was selling used cars out here. The next thing, Bill was selling used cars as a sub-agent. He had a store back then, one that sold appliances like gas-powered washing machines, radios that got signals from far away, refrigerators, and just about whatever you wanted. He would take the orders and have them shipped by train to Glenwood and bring them in from there. Bill was always at something, like building houses, and he had a lot of things on the go. I think his uncle helped him get started, but Bill was an enterprising type of man and he never stopped working.

"The next thing I knew Bill was after me to come work for him in Gander; that was about 1955 or so. He had built a garage, Bennett Motors, and was the Pontiac–Buick dealer in Gander. That was in addition to his appliance store. He was also the Hertz rental car franchisee back then. Anyway, I went to work for Bill because he promised he would get me a house to live in, and there weren't that many places to live in Gander at the time. He eventually did do just that, we made an arrangement to pay it out over time, and it's the same house I'm living in today some fifty years later.

"Bill could be difficult at times, he could be a hard man to work for because he would be up at 5 a.m. and work until late at night, and he expected everyone else to do the same, but you couldn't fault him for his dedication to his businesses. He was always treated with respect by everyone he dealt with and he treated them the same."

EDSEL LANGDON

Edsel Langdon is a long-time resident of Gander, a pilot who never flew for Bill's company, but once sold cars for Bill when he was in the used and new car business. He was a friend for years after, when Bill moved into the aviation business.

"I was on shift work and used to sell cars for him part-time," he said.

Edsel recalls that roads were not the best in those days, but it didn't prevent people from buying cars. Most of the roads were dirt at that time, not much pavement.

"You could go as far as Gambo on the east. Proceeding west from Gander you had two ferries to cross rivers, one on the Gander River at Glenwood, the other at Bishop's Falls on the Exploits River. This was long before they built bridges over those rivers."

Edsel has about forty years of flying under his belt, and it was Bill Bennett who gave him his float endorsement as a member of the Gander Flying Club in 1968. They used to fly together every now and then, but just as friends.

He remembered Bill's first plane, a Cessna 170. It was limited in what it could do and didn't have enough power. They later flew together to Toronto in it and traded it for a Cessna 180, a little better plane. That's before Bill had his commercial license.

Bill's first plane, Cessna 170.

"The 170 was getting tired, we needed a pretty big lake for takeoff with two people in it. Once the engine gets tired you lose the rpm's."

He recalled Jack Walsh and Bill going to Bogota, Columbia, in South America, to buy two De Havilland Beavers.

"They flew those planes all the way back to Gander and never had a problem. When you bid on those planes you never knew what you were going to get when you arrived there, but they were good ones. I remember when they arrived in Gander, they were in pretty good shape, but of course they had to go through full maintenance when they got back. You could get those planes then for next to nothing.

"The last time I spoke to him it was in November of 2000. He was getting a little bit shaky then, and I knew that through the years he had a number of small mini-strokes and I could see the change in him. I'm sure he had many more years left in him but it all caught up with him at the end.

"Flying all those years, he never had an accident," said Edsel. "That in itself was a great accomplishment."

MARY BENNETT

Mary (Mahoney) Bennett was born in Stock Cove, Bonavista Bay, in 1930. She met her future husband in Gander just after World War II, in 1946, and they were married in 1949. He was working with Trans Canada Airlines (TCA) at the time and she was a waitress in a local hotel.

It was through one of Bill's relatives, his great-aunt Mamie, that he acquired that first job. Her son, Walter Lawlor, was station manager at TCA, and he found work for the young man who would be assigned to loading and emptying freight or other chores.

Bill spent about six years with the company, she recalled. She remembered that well because they took advantage of a pass, which was only given to employees after five years of service, and flew to Vancouver for a trip. After they returned from that trip Bill began to work his way out of the airlines and into private business with an appliance store, selling automobiles, and he also had an auto rental business.

He was backed by a wealthy friend of the family, Jimmy King, who helped the young couple build a home in Gander. As a condition of the loan he would stay with them now and then when he was in town.

"I worked with Bill then when he got started with the rental car business, working in the office, cleaning out the cars and doing whatever had to be done. It was quite a lifestyle."

Despite their busy schedule, they still found time to have a family. Bill and Mary parented six children: Michael, Noel, Patrick, Cathy, Colleen, and Terri.

Later in this book you will find that four of Bill's children were influenced greatly by their father's aviation career. Noel became a highly respected bush pilot, Michael a supervisor in a large airline maintenance business, Terri worked with Eastern Provincial Airlines and later Canadian Airlines in Prince Edward Island for eighteen years, and Cathy was involved in meeting his guests in Labrador when they arrived to go sportfishing at his fishing lodges. The other children took different paths in their lives.

PART TWO
BUSH PILOTS: A BREED APART

IT TAKES A special breed of person to become a bush pilot. You have to have a love of flying first and foremost, an intimate knowledge of the aircraft and its limitations, a sense of adventure, a respect for nature and the weather, and a willingness to make decisions on a gut feeling that what you are doing is the right thing.

Bill Bennett had all of those qualities, and more. He had a business sense as well, and a caring nature that made friends easily and held them for a lifetime. He also had a sense of duty and of helping others less fortunate. He was a quiet and unassuming man until you crossed that imaginary line that only he knew, and then watch out.

He was a passionate conservationist, one who recognized the need for wise and sustained management of wildlife and fish stocks, and was not afraid to speak his mind to anyone who would listen, from the highest politician to the average man on the street. Most of all, he was an innovative aviator with a love of being in the sky. He loved to fly.

The following comments come from some of the other bush pilots who knew Bill or flew for him at one time or another, and of a dispatcher in Goose Bay who knows all of the pilots and their backgrounds.

MIKE BYRNE

A senior pilot for Labrador Airways and the float plane operations at Otter Creek, Mike Byrne has several decades of flying experience in the bush. He is now chief pilot on the Twin Otters and spends his summers flying these workhorses to the fishing lodges and to the mining sites farther north where exploration and the Voisey's Bay mine are active.

Mike began his career as an aircraft mechanic but was bitten by the flying bug and began flying in 1979. He now has close to thirty years and thousands of hours of flying time in Labrador under his belt.

In the early years he worked for Bill Bennett for several months before moving over to Eastern Provincial Airlines. His main flying job was delivering materials and goods by air to the Baie d'Espoir power project and flying goods into remote coastal communities such as Fogo Island.

Mike flew the fisheries contract for Bill in the summer from Makkovik, Labrador, and in the winter did the scheduled runs to service the coastal settlements of the island.

"He fired me a dozen times over the months I flew for him. One time I got caught up on a rock in Deadman's Pond and Bill had to come out in a boat to help get me off.

"'You're fired!' he told me. 'Get this load down to Baie d'Espoir and when you return you're through!'

"Of course, by the time I got back he'd cooled off and said he didn't mean it, I was still employed, but to be a little more careful next time. He was quick to react to things but cooled off just as fast and then it was all forgotten.

"I always had a lot of respect for Bill," Mike said. "He kept his planes in top notch condition and he had the finest fishing lodges in Labrador. I've flown into all of them at one time or another and his were always the best.

"Everybody in aviation knew of Bill Bennett and Gander Aviation. He knew the country and was a 'seat of your pants' pilot in many ways, one of the old-time bush pilots. He never took real chances because he always had a handle on the weather and knew how far he could get and where he could set down for a night if he had to.

"Many of the pilots of today flew at one time or another with Gander Aviation and learned their craft from Bill. He was one of a kind."

Bill at the site of his new garage.

LESTER POWELL

Lester Powell is a bush pilot who has been flying around Labrador since the 1960s, and his father Ben Powell is a Labrador pioneer settler who has written numerous books about his life on the Labrador coast. Lester was flying in the St. Anthony area during the time Bill had the Medivac contract for Sir Wilfred Grenfell Hospital. When it was necessary, Bill would replace a pilot and fly the missions himself.

One night they stayed overnight at the hospital facilities and he recalls Bill telling him a story about one guest who had concerns about being stuck at the Michael's River lodge because of bad weather that had hit the coast. Instead of waiting for the regular turnaround the following day, this fellow insisted on having a helicopter come in to get him and fly him out.

"This weather is going to pass overnight," Bill told the worried guest. "Tomorrow it's supposed to be clear and bright."

But no matter how much Bill tried to convince him, this chap wanted a helicopter in and he wanted it right now. Bill told him it would be at his own expense, but the guest didn't seem to mind, and Bill ended up calling out for a chopper to come in. The ceiling was very low and the only way the pilot could get there was to follow the coastline, with the water on one side of the aircraft and the land on the other. Of course this meant following the irregular coastline all the way from Goose Bay out Lake Melville, in every little cove and bay, so he had some reference point on the land.

He had to refuel at Rigolet and continued out to Michael's River, arriving sometime after supper. The guest was ready to go, but the pilot said it was too late, they would never get back in time before dark, and they would have to stay there overnight. Well, the guest had no choice then, so he and the pilot stayed overnight at the lodge.

The next morning Bill loaded the remaining guests and their gear aboard the single Otter and left the lone guest there with the helicopter pilot.

"We got back to Goose Bay in the Otter long before that guest and the helicopter pilot did!" Bill told Lester. "Some people just won't listen!"

There was another time in the late 1960s when Bill lost an engine while crossing Groswater Bay. It was rough, said Lester, and Bill eventually got the plane ashore by inching it in. He was there for quite awhile before a mechanic and some parts were flown in on another plane from Gander, and in-between he had some food dropped to him by Search & Rescue so he could survive.

Flying a bush plane in those days always had its dangers!

Jim Burton

Jim Burton is a highly successful real estate agent in the St. John's area and operator of Flower's River Lodge on the Flower's River in Labrador. Jim is also a pilot who owns a De Havilland Beaver and flies out of Goose Bay to service his lodge and transport his staff around.

Jim recalls the first time he became interested in aviation. His dad Vince worked for several years as Bill Bennett's accountant and office manager as the young business grew. Jim was a very young boy in Gander at the time. He was out by the float plane base at Deadman's Pond with his dad when Bill landed and taxied up to the dock. Jim stood on the dock as the plane landed and Bill asked him if he wanted to go for a ride.

He lifted Jim aboard the plane and took off, circling around the Gander area, and brought it in for a landing again. Jim was hooked on flying from that point onward.

I could see by the distant gaze and smile on his face as he told me the story that it was one of the highlights of his youth and what would prove to be the inspiration for his later life as a bush plane pilot.

KEN WATKINS

Ken flew for Bill Bennett for about 10 months in 1964. He came from Ontario and applied for the job with Bill when he was about 23, the junior pilot of four who were working for Gander Aviation at the time.

"When it was busy in the summer and fall all of us would be working, but once winter rolled in the other three went their separate ways while I stayed on and flew for the winter."

Once spring rolled around things slowed down, ice was getting rotten and it was time to change from skis to floats. There was not much work, so Ken decided to go to Eastern Provincial Airways and apply for a job with them. Royal Cooper, who flew in the Second World War and was a well-known pilot in the Gander area, told Ken that the planes Bill had in his fleet belonged to them, and part of their lease agreement with Bill was that they promised not to "steal" any of his pilots away from him.

"This is a touchy business," he told Ken, "but you're not flying with him now this spring and I would really like to have you flying for us, so tell you what we'll do. Why don't you go on back to Toronto and get your multi-engine endorsement, and take it easy for a bit, and I'll tell Bill you've decided to fly the Canso water bombers and need to get your endorsement. That way we won't really be stealing you from him."

"So I went back and told Bill I was going on the Canso, and he wasn't too happy about that."

"I taught you everything you know, and I'm not too fussy about letting you go, but I suppose if you're going to fly the Canso it will be a good move for you," Bill told him.

"So I was hired by EPA and when I came back I was put on the Beaver. Well, I was worried about Bill's reaction if he saw me, because the dock for EPA was right next to that of Gander Aviation on Deadman's Pond in Gander. But as luck would have it, I didn't run into him and I was told to go over to Pasadena and I would be based there, so I booted it off Deadman's Pond and was over on the west coast breathing a sigh of relief.

"Later that summer I had a call asking about the hours on the Beaver, and it was time for it to have a periodic inspection, so they told me to bring it back to Gander, which I did. When I landed and taxied into the EPA dock, there was Bill looking out his window as the plane reached the dock. I wondered if I could make it out of there without him seeing me, but the next thing I knew he spotted me, did a double take as if he couldn't believe his eyes, and came running out to the dock.

"'You!' he shouted. 'What are you doing back here flying for them? I taught you everything you know, and this is what I get for it! I'll get to the bottom of this; I'll talk to Royal Cooper and find out what's going on, you won't be staying over there!'

"Bill went on that rant for quite a bit, he was hopping mad, but he finally calmed down and it must have been straightened out because I was still flying for EPA afterward.

"Another time when we were flying equipment to the south

coast during development of the Baie d'Espoir power project, I was on my way out to take off on Deadman's Cove and got hung up on a rock. Bill came out in a boat, ranting and raving, helped me get off the rock, and then he told me I was fired as soon as I got back from this trip. Of course, by the time I returned he had cooled down and was pretty mellow.

"'You've got to be more careful next time,' he told me. 'You could have really damaged that float and put the plane out of commission for awhile and cost us a lot of money. You can forget about that business of firing you, I was just upset.'"

Bill was like that, Ken said. He would get all up tight and a few minutes later it was like nothing had ever happened.

Another time Ken had flown into Baie Verte during the winter. It was a clear day when he left Gander but the area was hit that evening with a vicious storm. He had the plane moored on a pond just outside Baie Verte and when he went out to get it the plane was buried in snow right to the top of the wings.

"I called Gander and told Bill about it, and he began fuming about getting it out of the snow, why couldn't I go and get some help in Baie Verte, and so forth. No matter what I said to him it seemed like he got madder, so eventually I got mad myself and told him he could come and get the plane himself, I was going to catch a bus back home to Deer Lake.

"'Now, now,' he tried calming me down, 'it's no good getting on like that.' But I was just so mad that I wouldn't listen. So he sent out Ernie, his chief aide and pilot at the time, and between us we dug it out and I flew it back to Gander.

"'You see,' said Bill, 'you should have been able to get that plane out of there, you have to be more careful, et cetera.' And finally Ernie piped up and told him there was no way anyone could have moved that plane, it was buried, and eventually he calmed down and accepted it. Of course, I stayed on with him.

"There was another time when Bill asked me to stop at his hunting camp on Little Gander Pond and pick up something. It was in winter and the snow was high, and there were two markers sticking up on the end of this dock. When I turned the plane to get out I must have accidentally caught the corner of the elevator on the post and tore a hole in the fabric.

"Bill was upset as usual. 'How in the hell did you do that? This will cost me a fortune to have repaired, you know! I'll have to send it over to EPA to get it fixed.' A few weeks later he came in and slapped an invoice on the table for $700, which was a good bit of money back then, and probably equivalent to about $15,000 these days.

"'Now,' he said, 'Now you see what that little accident cost me!'

"He wasn't mad about it. Bill knew these little things happened. You couldn't avoid them, but I guess he wanted to let me know the cost so we'd be more careful the next time.

"I kept flying for EPA until 1978 when I took a job with the provincial government supervising flight operations with Government Air Services. I flew again for one summer in 1979 but after that didn't fly much at all. One night in 1985, Bill called me out of the blue, and I hadn't heard from him in all those years. The wife and I had our bags packed ready to go on holidays the next morning. Bill told me he had a problem and asked me to fly the fisheries contract in Labrador that summer. All flights had to be approved through my office and I knew he had the contract, but he was in a spot with no one to fly that contract.

"'I haven't flown in 5 or 6 years,' I told him, 'and I would be in a conflict of interest because of my government job.'

"Bill said, 'Don't you worry about that stuff. I'll take care of that, you just get over to Deadman's Pond in the morning and Glenn Goobie will give you a few turns around the lake to check you out.'

"I talked it over with my wife, and she told me to go ahead if I wanted, we could have our holiday anytime. So I called him and told him I would do it for him, it was six weeks to two months on that fisheries contract.

"When I got to Deadman's Pond the next day, there were four guys waiting on the dock with toolboxes and suitcases and all sorts of heavy gear.

"'Oh, yes, on your way I need you to drop off these four fellows at Black Tickle,' Bill told me. Knowing that it was a heavy load, Bill told me that we could move through the narrows and get out onto the larger pond so I would have enough room to take off without any problems. So Bill went out in his boat and told me to follow him through the narrows to avoid the few rocks.

Traversing rapids in a Gander River boat.

"I was following him out, but there was a good wind on and I figured I had enough room to get off without going into the big pond, so at the last minute I turned and fired her up. Bill turned and looked, did a double take, and later I learned that he figured we were all going to be killed. But I got off the water with plenty of room and headed up to the Labrador coast.

"When I got to Black Tickle there was lots of ice in the harbour and I was worried about hitting a chunk and tearing off a float, but I found a clear area and got her down okay, booted those four fellows and their gear off the plane, and got out again before the ice closed in on me.

"I went on to Goose Bay and later got a call from Bill who told me I did okay, he figured I would be fine. Bill must have taken care of everything politically as well because I still had my job afterward and never heard anymore about it.

"There was another time when he had a pilot named Chuck Ellsworth flying for him. He had done something wrong and Bill had suspended him for a couple of weeks, and then on his first day back Bill sent him off to Clarenville for a stop and then on to some other destination farther west.

"About an hour later I was in the office when the phone rang and it was the pilot on the other end. 'This is Charles Ellsworth calling,' he said. 'You can tell Mr. Bennett that his Cessna 185 is sitting upside down in the harbour. All that's sticking up are the floats.'

"I asked him what happened and he just said he'd lost control on landing. He was okay, but the plane was there upside down. Then I said, 'You know, Mr. Bennett is not going to be very happy about this!'

"'Yes, I know. You can tell him I'll pack my bags as soon as I get back!'"

Ken summed it up this way. "All in all, Bill was a fine

man. I learned a lot from him, had a great summer doing that contract, and always had a great deal of respect for him and what he accomplished.

"He built the best lodges in the province and took care of all his planes. Bill could be very emotional at times, and when he was upset you had to take him with a grain of salt, because when it was over he was the best kind.

"A lot of pilots who came up through Gander Aviation moved on to some big jobs with other airlines, very well-trained as pilots, and it was all thanks to Bill Bennett."

RICK DAWE

Rick Dawe has been a dispatcher with several airline companies in Happy Valley-Goose Bay and is currently with Provincial Airlines in that capacity. A native of Gander, he grew up with memories of Bill Bennett flying in and out of the float-plane base at Deadman's Pond on his missions to places in remote areas of the province.

"As a boy I would be fishing at Deadman's Pond during the summer months, and there was always a lot of activity with his planes flying in and out. You could tell they were Gander Aviation by the orange and white colours of his planes.

"During those early days in Gander, Bill and Gander Aviation were quite prominent. Bill pushed it along and kept it growing, he had a knack for getting customers and contracts."

When Rick moved to Goose Bay to work with the bush plane companies he got to know Bill even better. At Otter Creek he was responsible for booking schedules to the various outfitting lodges and often became involved in heated discussions with some of the operators due to cancellations because of inclement weather or aircraft maintenance. Bill was no stranger to these situations.

"Bill always had a quick temper. He would argue his points and then it was out of his system and over with. Once he calmed down it was like it never happened. He knew there was nothing I could do about weather and maintenance, they were beyond my control, but he was concerned about moving his guests in and out and I couldn't blame him."

Rick considers Bill one of the best bush pilots he ever knew – and he knew most of them at one time or another.

"He was an old-time pilot; he knew the capacity of his aircraft and what they were capable of handling, and their characteristics when flying with a load. I recall one evening when I was at Otter Creek, the weather was bad with a northeast wind, the ceiling was low and everyone had gone home because nothing was flying. I was just closing up when I heard the sound of an aircraft engine in the distance, and out of the night appeared Bill Bennett in his Beaver. He circled and landed, so I helped him secure the plane.

"I asked what in the world he was doing out on a night like this. Bill told me he was at his lodge in Michael's River and had watched the weather coming down. When he figured it was about as bad as it could possibly get, he decided he could still make it into Goose Bay by flying down Lake Melville, so he took off. He knew from experience what it was like on the way in and he knew the capability of his plane."

Another time they were chatting about the company and what Bill had achieved in terms of his success.

"'What are you going to do with all your money? Why don't you go out and buy yourself a yacht?' I asked him jokingly.

"'I don't need to buy a yacht, I have my three yachts right

here in Labrador at Michael's River, Sandhill River and Wulff Lake. Those are my yachts. My dream all my life was to have these places. Why would I want or need a yacht?'

"Bill catered to everyone and that's what made him a success," Rick said. "He was always looking for new clients, even bringing in some British and European fishermen over the years. Like I said, he had that knack of attracting customers."

Rick figures that Bill's real love was the outdoors of the province, from his hunting camps and lodge on the island to his three lodges in Labrador.

"He loved being in the outdoors, living that life, and he loved catering to people. I think flying was just a means of getting there and doing those things. He was a real pioneer in both bush plane aviation and in outfitting."

PART THREE
THE LEGACY LIVES ON

NOEL BENNETT

Noel Bennett is Bill's youngest son, and in 2007 was Chief Pilot for Provincial Airlines and based in Goose Bay, Labrador. He left a job flying Boeing 727-200 jets for First Air to return to Goose Bay six years previously because of his love for the lifestyle and outdoors of Labrador.

He began with flying Twin Otters and ended landing the huge 200,000 pound, 727 jets in some strange places, such as ice fields in Iqualuit.

Noel remembers being brought to Labrador and his father's fishing lodges when he was only a young boy, flying up from Gander with his father and spending his summers helping out at the camps in Michael's River and Sandhill River. When guests asked him what the summer weather was like back in Gander, he couldn't tell them because he was never there.

"When we were three or four we'd probably go up for a week or two with Mother, then when we turned six or seven we would go up for the summer, most of the time we'd be at

Michael's River. There were other things to do there, not like being stuck in a fishing camp in the middle of nowhere. We could walk the beaches and do a little fishing and so forth. When we got to be ten or eleven years old we'd do things like a cook's helper or making beds and things, like a child labour camp [here he chuckled].

"After you got to be about sixteen or so you began to be paid. From cook's helper you'd go off at fourteen or fifteen to work with the guides and help them out, and at sixteen or so you'd be a guide yourself. When I was a little older I was the camp manager, because although I was only a young kid I had been around it all my life and I knew about the generators and the camp operation and how it all worked. I would run the camp until I was about eighteen and then I went to flying school in Moncton. I worked there in Labrador for the summer that first year, went back to the flying school in the fall, and the following summer I began flying the planes for Dad. I was about nineteen or twenty then. Now I could fly the airplanes, too.

"There was one time when I was at Sandhill and I had to fly into Goose Bay to pick up some guests, so I took the river boat down to the mooring where the plane was tied on, tied off the boat there and got into the plane and flew into Goose Bay. I still had my rubber boots on from being in the boat, so I picked up the guests and carried them down to Otter Creek and was loading their gear aboard the plane and one of them asked me who the pilot was.

"'I'm flying the plane, I'm your pilot,' I told them. So I flew them out to Sandhill and we got off the plane and I got them into the boat.

"'Who's going to take us up the river?' one asked. 'I'm taking you up the river,' I told him. So we got going up the river and I stopped at the first pool where I knew there were a lot of fish. 'There's lots of salmon in the river,' I told them. 'This is a good pool if you'd like to stop here and fish for a bit.'

"So one asked me who was going to be their guide, and I told them, 'I'm your guide,' so they fished for awhile and caught a couple of salmon that we brought up to the camp.

"Once I got them into the camp the cook came out and told me he was having some trouble with the generator, so I told them to settle in, I had to go up and check out the generator problem, but to relax and I would be back soon and we could go out fishing. I got the generator fixed and when I returned there were a lot of raised eyebrows.

"One of them asked me, 'Do all the guides fly the plane too?'

"I told him, 'No sir, just me.'

"It was those many years of working with my dad as a boy and learning how the camps worked that gave me the experience to do all those things, you know. Even as a very young man I had been well-trained, so it was all a part of me."

He recalls hearing that his father had a lot of camps back in the 1960s before Noel was even born. Camp 836 was one, also known as Dollard's Pond, then there was Sitdown Pond, and there were also a lot of tent camps.

"Most of those were operating before I was born, but every place there was fish or moose or caribou, he knew about them and where they were located.

"The Conne River Band wanted to buy the camp at Dollard's Pond and Bill didn't want to sell it, but they threatened to build a place right next door to him and so he got rid of it and sold it.

"Then he decided he would build a place at Sitdown Pond, so got all the paperwork done and began to fly in materials. The Indians found out he was building there and they decided they wanted one there as well, and began to build it on one of the other shores.

Bill and guide with a trophy caribou.

Bill the outfitter (centre) with a nice moose.

"Well, Dad was fit to be tied, but they had to come to him to fly their materials in, so he went along with it and flew in all their materials. Then the government got wind of what they were doing and they shut down the Indians from building there because Dad already had the permits. So there they were, with a pile of building materials on the beach and no permit to build, and they had to take it all out again.

"Well, rather than do that, Dad offered to take it off their hands and he bought it all from them, so essentially they had paid all the costs of shipping his materials into the lake. He was pretty shrewd.

"He said, 'They might have beat me on 836, but they didn't beat me on Sitdown Pond!'

"The only thing is they had all their materials on the other side of the lake and he had to move them over, but it wasn't too hard a pill to swallow.

"Bill Anstey was telling me a story, they were in the Otter and they landed on skis at 836 one evening and spent the night at the camp. They had left the beacon light on, but they got to having a few drinks and nobody noticed it. The next morning when they got up and went down to the plane the battery was dead, so they couldn't start the plane. They had no radio to get in touch with anyone to let them know where they were and what had happened, so all they could do was sit there and wait for someone to come in and find them. They were also feeling a bit guilty and wondering how they were going to explain everything to Bill.

"So the next morning they hear a plane coming in and it lands out near the Otter, which was a good ways down the lake from the camp. They got dressed and began to walk down toward the plane, trying to get their story straight, and figuring Bill was going to take a strip off them. Before they reached the Otter, the Cessna took off again, and they couldn't figure out what had happened. When they reached the Otter, there was a new battery lying in the snow.

"It appears Dad had figured out what happened and was so poisoned he didn't want to talk to them! He just dropped off the battery and left without saying a word."

Noel feels that you must like the outdoors and the out-door life to fly in the bush in the Canadian North. "There's nothing like listening to the sounds of loons or seeing a beautiful lake as far as I'm concerned."

He's landed in some strange places in his years as a bush pilot.

"In some places a fjord may be nestled beneath mountains that are up to 10,000 feet in altitude, and our passengers would be climbers who wanted to be dropped off at the bottom and begin at the base. It would take us fifteen minutes sometimes to get the plane back up to altitude and you had the wind funneling down through that gorge to contend with."

He remembered his dad at the Gander base working in the office, catching up with the never-ending paperwork before leaving for Labrador. He would have his staff standing by to leave with him, maybe guides or cooks for the camps, and when he finally had the paperwork completed then he would be ready to leave.

"There would be hardly enough daylight left to get very far, but he would load them all aboard and take off to get as far as he could. He would leave knowing that there wasn't enough daylight, but his idea was that if he could get off Newfoundland and reach the Labrador coast, then he would have got that far and that was good enough for now.

"You'd never end up in a town. If the weather was not good we'd get as far as we could, then he'd land at a lake where there was probably a small cabin, and there was always lots of food aboard the plane, so he and the guides would get under shelter and have a meal, probably a few drinks, and he'd say, 'We've got it pretty good, don't we boys?'

"We'd never end up in a town because he'd have to put everyone up in a motel or hotel, so we'd stay in the country and poke on the next day. He'd be under pressure to get the camps open so the important thing was getting to the Labrador side. He knew the land so well that there was usually no problem finding a place to stay for the night.

"He was a conservationist, whether or not he knew it. Dad was passionate about things. He didn't want to see anything wasted, like people catching trout by the hundreds and then throwing them out in the spring where you'd find them out on the dump.

"Once he was in a plane and flying, his mood changed. He was away from the phones and the pressures, and he became peaceful up in the air. These days out in the bush it is so easy to communicate that he wouldn't be happy. And as much as he liked being out in the country at the lodges, it wasn't that good for his business because he couldn't be back there at the office to take care of things and to find more work for his planes.

"I remember one time when I flew out to Sandhill with my buddy and had left my fishing rod in Goose Bay. I called into Goose to see if anyone might be coming out that way, and if they could drop it off. So a few days later we were fishing up at Northwest Brook just off the Sandhill when this plane came in. It was Father and he spotted us fishing there, so he landed and taxied the plane up to where we were, opened the door, and called out, 'So you forgot your rod, did you?' He passed it over to me, smiled, and took off again – just like that."

Noel spent most of the summer flying for his father, but in the fall went to work with a company in Blanc Sablon,

Quebec, because he wanted to fly year round. He had his career planned, he wanted to be a pilot, and this was work for him in the winter months.

"Father wasn't too impressed that I was going to work with another company, but by the next summer he's gotten over it and I spent the summer flying for him in Labrador. I did that for a few years. I got to go salmon fishing every few days in the summer and had the best of both worlds for a few years. The deal was that the company in Blanc Sablon wanted to lease Dad's Beaver in the fall for moose and caribou hunting, so he agreed to do that as long as he could have me and the Beaver back flying for him in the summer months. That was the trade-off."

At one time Bill had up to twelve or thirteen aircraft in the Gander Aviation fleet, including two DC-3s.

"Dad had a contract to do cable patrol, where the planes would patrol over the Trans-Atlantic Cable and make sure there were no boats fishing in the area. They would drop pamphlets in several languages, some of which landed on the boats, telling them they weren't allowed to fish there with their draggers and nets because they could tangle up in the cable.

"The planes weren't built with a cargo door, they only had a passenger door, so there was a limit to what they could do. They weren't any good for transporting freight."

Of all of Bill's children, it is Noel who has followed in his father's footsteps as a bush pilot with a love of the land and of the skies above. His passion for the North is at least as strong as that of his father, and at the young age of 37, he has already amassed years of experience in flying the North.

There is plenty of time remaining to add to the legend of the Bennett name in the annals of Newfoundland and Labrador aviation.

MICHAEL BENNETT

Michael Bennett is Bill's eldest son, and in 2007, he was a supervisor with IMP Aerospace in Halifax, a large aircraft maintenance company. Mike worked at the huge hangar near the Robert L. Stanfield airport in Halifax. His memories go back to the late 1950s and early 1960s when his father first got out of Bennett Motors and began flying big game hunters into the interior.

"Dad had a bush plane operation at Deadman's Pond near Gander. He had built a very basic camp at Mt. Peyton, just some tents on platforms to begin with, and that's how he got started with catering to hunters. He used his small plane as a hopper, he was there in 20 minutes or so. He used Eastern Provincial Airlines (EPA) to bring hunters into Gander and then took them out from there. He started that in the early 1960s and it lasted for a couple of years, but it was a short-lived season, only lasting from October to November. Dad had some politicians on his side and always got whatever licenses he needed each year. He bought them in a lot and paid for them, and then it was up to him to sell them to the hunters. Whatever he didn't sell – well, he was out of luck because they wouldn't take them back.

"There were a lot of isolated communities back then that needed to get supplies and materials once the winter set in, and people needed to get out for medical procedures and the like, so he got into that type of work because EPA, who had small planes and was doing that at the time, wanted to get into turbo prop aircraft and out of the bush plane business.

"So he started a charter service. Dad went out and got a few more small planes, got a few more small camps built in the woods, did most of his own flying. EPA finally got out altogether and Dad took over the flying into the outports and flying into the dam at Baie d'Espoir where a new hydro electrical facility was being built. He hired most of his guides out of Conne River, the Mi'kmaq, to get animals for his guests. Bill kept them working as much as possible, stayed with the hunting as main core. Fishing had too much road access at the time so he stayed away from that, but operated the hunting parts until the late 1980s.

"By the late 1960s his company was well established. It was about then that we experienced heavy ice situations along the coast, and much colder winters, which was not unusual for the early 1970s. We really had little to do in the winter up until then, the floats came off in fall and we converted them to ski-equipped planes. With the ice interruptions, we ended up taking care of places where ferries could not reach the communities in winter.

"It was either us or helicopters, and they were expensive, plus they couldn't carry the loads that we could. For about the next ten years we ran the planes from late fall to late spring, servicing the outport communities which were ice-bound. It was the passengers who had to pay the price of the plane. We would go to Fogo, about 30 minutes in and 30 minutes back out. The mail was secured first and had to be delivered as priority, food went on next, and booze was last. We would be on a steady go back and forth on a daily basis. Sometimes we'd load up at night, with the pilot, usually Dad, ready to go at first light.

"Eventually fuel was built up for the island. There was time to get fuel tankers in and fuel stored to heat stoves and for other uses like running chainsaws and snowmobiles. We would fly Christmas catalogues out for people to order gifts, and return with them in the mail bags. Dad hated to carry beer because it was too heavy and cumbersome. He would sometimes stay overnight at the hotel if it was late, flying out early the next morning, moving cargo and people back and forth. It wasn't a 9 to 5 job. We flew from daylight to dark, and might do fifteen trips a day due to the short distances. Down at Deadman's Pond we had a big warehouse, unheated, but in the morning when the pilots arrived the planes would all be loaded and warmed up, ready to go.

"Dad went to the politicians and pleaded for them to come up with some help for the families out there who had to pay for the tickets to get back and forth to the mainland and finally saw a change. Government came up with a subsidy for passengers to travel to the isolated outports, covering about 50% of tickets.

"He obtained the ambulance service as well, using a Turbo Beaver for the Medivac. The only way to reach these areas was either helicopter or float plane. Dad told government that they needed some small runways because he sometimes had to land and take off on thin ice. It was very dangerous at times when breakup was occurring, but he had to deliver the goods. He asked the politicians, 'Help me build a runway,' and eventually got a gravel runway built on Fogo Island, the first runway there. This enabled him to land when the ice was bad and he needed to get in with the ambulance service. The government eventually took over with Air Services.

"At one point we had up to twelve aircraft, including a couple of DC-3 dual engine planes that we used for the Trans-Atlantic Cable Patrol contract to check cable links from Newfoundland to Europe. We tried it with two Queen Airs, but realized that we needed bigger planes because we would go out for six to seven hours at a time and cover up to the 200-mile limit. If a dragger hooked into cable by accident it would disrupt communications for days or weeks, so we would fly out based on a report or on a schedule maybe three days a week.

"If we did see a ship in our travels and it was heading for the cable, we would fly over and get her registration, then drop pamphlets warning them that they were working in the vicinity of the cable and if something became severed no one would be talking between Europe and North America until those cables were repaired. Messages were written on waterproof paper and in all languages, rolled up like a tube. We took pictures of the ship and flew over it to drop those pamphlets from the plane, and they got the message that they were fishing in the vicinity of the cable.

"The two DC-3s did the work on that contract for five to six years and did the job better than Queen Airs. As improvements in communications got better the cable system became obsolete. The old cable was still there but not used like in the past, so we lost the contract because it wasn't needed anymore. Newfoundland continued to improve; we got more roads and other services, and the result was that we lost some of the aircraft business as technology grew, and people began to drive rather than fly at the considerably higher cost.

"Dad constructed more small hunting camps, but there was lots of competition on the west coast and many changes took place. I told him we had to continue to promote hard and meet that competition. We did a few sportsmen shows, but if no bookings came out of it he never went back to the same show the following year. But I think he did learn that he needed to market and promote. Dad did not like change, but he had to conform.

"Dad went to Labrador back in the 1970s. He still had small planes to handle fall hunting and in the winter it was servicing outports; he did a lot of charters up there and did a couple of shows with CBC about flying in the bush. In those days he was flying with a compass because there were no beacons in place then. Dad did a lot of work for the Department of Public Works; they were building docks and an infrastructure, and he was flying in supplies. So he flew back and forth doing charters and developing wharfs and services in the Labrador outports. There was a bit of sport-fishing going on but not a great deal back then, and he formed a new passion to develop a fishing camp.

"He landed at Michael's River one day by himself, checked it out, and decided to build a lodge there. Later we stopped there for the night and slept in the plane; we had fishing rods on board and couldn't believe what we were catching: big Arctic char and Atlantic salmon and sea trout. He recognized the potential to lure people into the area for this kind of fishing.

"He saw an old shack and was ready with sandwiches and lunch when an Inuit came down with his rifle to see what was going on. 'This doesn't look good!' I thought to myself. I figured he was thinking, 'My place, my area, now I have a white man here!'

"Dad went up to the old shack, brought some stuff with him and had talks with the Inuit. He must have made peace with him, it looked like no one was going to be shot, and he just wanted to know what the plane was doing there. The next year Bill had his mind made up to talk to hunters and ask, 'Why not come with me to Labrador?' He had tent camps put up on platforms, hired some guides from Conne River, built the camp and got some hunters to join him.

"He bought a lot of gear, which we had shipped up on CN Marine. They dropped it off the coast at Byron Bay, including groceries, food, gas, boats and motors. It was time to put up a real place. But we needed a better site, so we built across the river on a hill. I went up after school let out in June and worked hard. I washed every dish, peeled potatoes, did whatever he wanted done, and was back at end of summer when school began.

"Dad decided to build a better place, so he got some carpenters hired, drew up plans, and ordered materials for the next year. They poured concrete pillars and began. The time of night was not important; it stayed light until very late and we worked long hours. We got our stuff unloaded on large boats and began building a quality lodge. It was booked solid, there were lots of fish and the business began. We had generators, a fully equipped kitchen, dining room, three bedrooms, and took six guests to start – mostly Americans and foreigners from Europe, very few Canadians. We then built guide quarters. We had two Beavers that had been bought in Bogota to fly in more materials for the continued construction.

"Guests had their limit caught in a few hours. In those days they kept the fish, and the only way to keep them fresh was to cover them up in snowbanks. We'd place them in a freezer temporarily to stiffen up and then store them in the snowbanks that were close to the lodge almost all summer long.

"Things were going so well that Dad decided to build an expansion, and our guides were required to work extra hours after guiding to dig out a cellar and increase the occupancy for up to ten guests from six. When he tried to put in that cellar, everyone quit on him. They told him that's not what they were hired to do and refused to dig out the sand. He finally had some other people come in for labour and got the cellar built; they mixed concrete and poured it there on site, a major job!

"He brought in carpenters and electricians, plumbers, and trades people to do the work required. Some of the guests came back ten to fourteen years in a row, and he wanted to cater to them so he built an extra piece on. Later he wanted to build a luxury place, so he added two suites for couples who now and then had come in, and the accommodations were immaculate. At the end of the day he had built a lodge 140' long and with a capacity for twelve guests.

"When that building spurt calmed down he had it pretty well balanced. Guests were still coming in and bookings were solid, and the flying was going good. Of course the guests wanted to fish all the time and guides didn't get much rest; they were on a 'steady go' for seven days a week. About three years later things became a little quieter, and he had built other lodges at Sandhill River to accommodate guests, so that was keeping him pretty well occupied, but I think Michael's River was always his favourite place."

CATHY (BENNETT) MITCHINSON

Bill's eldest daughter Cathy spent one summer working for her father in Goose Bay, meeting and greeting guests who were inbound on commercial airlines en route to the various lodges. She would meet their planes as they landed in Goose Bay, drive them to a hotel, make arrangements for their pickup the following morning, and pick up any supplies they might want to bring out with them on the float plane.

Bill had constructed a building at Otter Creek where the float planes docked and fueled, and that's where Cathy spent most of her off time, working the communications and ensuring the guests were taken care of. It was quite a change from her usual haunts in Canada's largest city, Toronto, but she enjoyed it immensely.

There were times when she and her dad didn't see eye to eye, and she usually let it slide when he said something she didn't agree with, but there was one time that summer when she stood up to him.

"Everything got quiet on the other end of the fringe radio after I spouted off, and I had no idea what he was thinking. Here was I, his daughter, barking back at him, and it was the first time I can remember ever having the courage to speak my mind.

"It seemed like a very long time before he came back on, and he was trying to hold back his laughter. I could hear it in his voice. He told me it was okay, to do it my way, and I think he was proud that I had the gumption to stand up to him on this issue."

When Bill passed away, Cathy caught the first plane to Newfoundland and on the flight she wrote a eulogy to her father. It can be found in the final part of this book.

Cathy was a lot like her dad. She respected convention, but when the church told her she could not read the eulogy at the funeral service it got her back up. At a point in the service when the priest had his back turned to the parishioners and was busy at the altar, she jumped up and took her place at the podium and delivered her message.

"What could they say or do at that point?" she later commented. "By God, I wanted to give that eulogy and nothing or no one was going to stop me."

She is her father's daughter, that's for sure. It was something Bill would have done.

PART FOUR
STAFF AND FRIENDS' MEMORIES

OVER THE YEARS, when he operated his hunting and fishing camps, Bill often employed residents of Conne River, a Mi'kmaq community in southern Newfoundland. The residents had grown up fending for themselves by living off the land and were superb woodsmen. Always hard workers, many of them worked at the island hunting camps in the fall and the Labrador fishing camps for the summer months. The following are the stories of Mi'kmaq guides Aloysius Benoit, Melvin McDonald, Pius John, and Aden McDonald.

ALOYSIUS "WISH" BENOIT

Bill employed several guides over the years who were residents of Conne River, now the only status Indian reserve in the province. Their experience of living off the land made them excellent employees at the camps, and their knowledge about moose, black bear, caribou and salmon kept the guests happy.

One who worked for him for a few years was Aloysius "Wish" Benoit, in his late 80s at the time of writing. Wish worked as a hunting guide on the island of Newfoundland at some of the tent camps that Bill had going at the time in places like Deer Pond and Dollard's Pond.

Wish said Bill was very particular when it came to respecting the animals. If a moose was hit by a bullet, you had to find it no matter how long it took. He didn't want any animals wounded and left to die.

Bill would work from daylight to dark, said Wish, and all the guides were expected to do the same.

He recalled the time when Bill was running late and was returning to the main operation at Dollard's Pond just before darkness settled in. "Did you leave those lights on at the point like I asked you to before we left?" Bill asked him. "Yes, I did like you told me," Wish replied.

"I didn't know at the time why he wanted those lights going in daylight but I soon found out. As we approached the pond it was very dark and you could hardly see anything, but those lights on the point were as clear as could be. Bill just cruised in and set the plane down on the pond just like it was a sunny day. We followed the lights into the beach and everything was perfect."

Melvin McDonald

Melvin McDonald, another guide from Conne River, began guiding for Bill in 1967 at a tent platform hunting camp that he helped set up at Round Pond on August 20. He was guiding for black bear and moose for the most part. He worked at Meddonagonix Lake and at Dollard's Pond on the island and spent one summer at Michael's River and another at Sandhill River before giving up the guiding business. Now a successful businessman, he owns and operates a large grocery outlet in Conne River.

"I always found Bill Bennett to be a good man to work for. He treated everyone fairly and let you do your job."

Bill circa 1969.

PIUS JOHN

One of Bill's long-time guides at the fishing lodges in Labrador was a Mi'kmaq Indian from Conne River by the name of Pius John. He began his outdoor career as a very young man of sixteen, back in 1947, guiding at a hunting camp on Little Ridge.

Pius spent more than twenty years working for Bill, from 1970 to 1991, first at Michael's River and eventually at Sandhill. Pius returned year after year because he was always treated with respect and trust by Bill Bennett.

A quiet man, Pius shared some of his experiences with me during an interview at Conne River in August of 2007. Long since retired, he still had vivid and fond memories of his jobs with Bill.

At Michael's River he and another Conne River guide, Melvin McDonald, were charged with digging out a basement beneath the lodge. Bill was determined that he was going to pour a concrete basement beneath the main lodge, but the earth had to be removed first.

"I told Bill it wasn't going to be easy. The lodge was built on a sandy beach at the mouth of the river, and as we removed the sandy soil it kept foundering in. 'Keep at it,' Bill would say, 'we'll get it done.' But it seemed we could never get ahead of the game; the more we dug the more it foundered. I wasn't there the next year, he moved me to Sandhill, so I don't know how it came out, but I heard that it was done eventually."

[Author's note: Indeed it was. The first time I visited Michael's there was a full poured concrete foundation beneath it, with high walls and several rooms for storage areas.]

"Little things sometimes would upset Bill. One time we found a small length of green rope alongside the river, the type used by fishermen for their nets. Bill wondered where it came from because we didn't have anything like it at the camp, and someone made a comment that it could have been from a poacher's net. Bill was not too happy about that. It may have washed down from the camps at Wulff Lake above us, which was owned by some military higher-ups who had been stationed at Goose Bay at one time or another, but it really got his curiosity going. It was that sort of thing that he got upset with.

"One time we were sitting around talking. There was Harry Steele, Bill and myself, and Harry asked Bill how old he was. Bill didn't answer; he turned to me and asked, 'How old are you, Pius?' 'Fifty-eight,' I told him. 'Right on,' Bill said, 'that's how old I am!'

"You never knew whether or not to believe him, and I don't think many people knew what Bill's real age was. He was right, though, we were both fifty-eight at that time, but I don't think Harry really believed him."

There was one time that Pius remembered Bill coming into the lodge with his face covered in oil.

"He had some kind of oil leak in the motor of the plane. It kept coming back until it covered the windshield on the plane and he couldn't see, so he stuck his head out the window so he could see where he was going. Of course the oil washed back over his face, but he got the plane in all right and later repaired it. The leak was caused by a connection that had come loose, maybe because of the engine vibrations."

Pius and Bill were going down the Sandhill one day in a river boat and Pius asked Bill to use the push pole to keep them off the rocks if he saw one in the path of the boat. Bill had just reached down to pick up the pole when they struck a rock that tipped the boat on its side and pitched them both over the gunwale and into the river. The boat never tipped completely over, so they came up and grabbed it, climbed aboard, and, soaking wet, continued down to where the plane was moored.

Once they arrived, Bill took off his clothing and wrung it out, put it back on, fired up the plane and flew into Goose Bay as though nothing had happened. Pius remembers that he flew in his bare feet, his socks and boots were so wet that he left them off.

Another time Pius found a rod and case down at the landing where the plane came in. It was leaning against a tree by the beginning of the boardwalk that extended from the cove where the plane was moored all the way up to the Sandhill Lodge, several miles in total. Pius had no idea who the rod belonged to but he carried it up to the lodge and hid it beneath his bed, waiting for someone to claim it.

Bill's good friend Harold Penney came in a few days later and was commenting that he couldn't fish because Bill had lost his rod somewhere and couldn't find it. Pius asked him what the rod was like, and Harold described it to a "T." Pius brought it out from its hiding place under his bed.

"I found this one down leaning on a tree by the boardwalk," Pius told him, "and was waiting for someone to claim it. Here's your rod.

"Harold was elated that he had his rod and promptly went out to the river that evening and caught a nice salmon. I don't know if he ever told Bill about it.

"Bill wasn't above having a bit of fun with the guests at times. He didn't get to fish a great deal, he was so busy, but one night we were out on the river and Bill hooked a small salmon. He had an old rod and reel, and on the sixth cast he had this fish on. He played it for awhile but lost it, but when he returned to the camp he told this story about the huge salmon he had hooked and lost because the old rod and reel were no good for a fish of that size. I never told anyone the difference.

"Another thing about Bill, if the fishing was slow and no one had caught a salmon during their stay, he never let them go home empty-handed. He would fly out to the coast and go to a fish plant where the commercial fishermen were selling their salmon; some of them were real brutes, and he would come back to the lodge with eight or ten of the biggest kind for the guests to take home with them.

"And for the guides and cooks, if there was anything you needed or wanted he would bring it in for you on his next trip. He always treated me well, every once in awhile he would call me aside and tell me there would be a little extra in the pay this week but don't mention it to the rest of the guides. He could have done the same for all of them, I don't know, but as long as I did my job he seemed to be happy enough."

ADEN MCDONALD

Aden McDonald operated the hunting camps that the Conne River Band operated for many years and told of the time Bill was in Conne River to drop off three trappers at a pond back in the country.

"Whenever the plane landed, there would always be a crowd of young people around, so this one time he asked them if they wanted to go for a ride in the plane and if so, to climb aboard. The plan was to drop the three men in the country and then return to Conne River to bring the kids back."

Aden and the band chief went along to chaperone the kids so the plane was full. Bill dropped off the three men but struck a rock with the float and tore a good-sized gash in it on the way out. He returned to shore and tried jamming things down in the tear to seal it long enough to get off the water, but nothing worked. They eventually tried with all the passengers on one side to get weight off the bad float, but that didn't help either.

"Finally, Bill dropped us back on the shore and told us he had to leave us there for awhile; he was going to the next pond to get some tools to repair the damage, and he finally got the plane off. It had so much water in the float that it looked like a water bomber releasing a load over a fire!

"Once he got off the water and airborne, he made a turn and I figured he was going into Gander to have it fixed. I guess it was worse than he figured he could get repaired in the country. The chief and I got comfortable with the kids and prepared to spend the night. The next morning Bill showed up bright and early with the float repaired and we all got back without a problem. Bill had called the band office after he left and told them if anyone was missing a kid and wondering where they were, they were with us and spending the night in the country, and not to worry, he'd have us all back in the morning.

"Bill was highly respected for his compassion for kids and he would take them for a spin whenever he was in the community and had the time to do it. He was a great pilot as well, and knew the country as well as anyone could."

VINCE BURTON

Vince first began working for Bill Bennett in 1959. He moved from Grand Falls to Gander and his first job was with Bennett's home appliances business.

The newspaper ad that he answered read "house provided." It was a factor in his decision because it was hard to find a place to live in Gander at the time. Once he and his wife arrived he learned that the house was not yet available and he had to rent for several months, but the job turned out to be good and he was happy with the position. He and Bill hit it off right away. These are some of his comments.

"Bill was a very young man when he began his business career, in his late teens or early twenties. Just prior to that he had operated a garage, Bennett Motors, on the Trans Canada Highway, and had sold it. The car business was in a bit of decline at the time, but he still had a car rental business going.

"My job was office management, accountant, administrative assistant, and whatever. We operated from that Trans Canada site for about a year, but then moved up into the town and put up a building on Airport Road. Bill was really into that appliances business in a big way.

"I can remember loading up Bill's truck with washers, stoves, refrigerators, you name it, and it would come back empty almost every night. The salesman would come back with a fistful of financial contracts with IAC, the International Acceptance Corporation, and the next day would be off again.

"About 1960 or 1961 Bill got his private license and bought a Cessna 170 aircraft. Then we sold that building on Airport Road and moved the operations down to Deadman's Pond. We had a building there and we expanded on it, and that's where we eventually operated the airline.

"Shortly after that, Bill got his commercial license and formed Gander Aviation. We went into the commercial business, flying people everywhere. The fleet slowly increased from the Cessna to a Beaver, an Otter, and other aircraft.

"The big thing in the mid-1960s was the Baie d'Espoir hydroelectric development, and we flew all the materials there for that big project. Most of the flying was done by the single-engine Otter, and we had the contract to carry passengers and mail into Fogo on the scheduled service. The mid-1960s were busy times for us.

"Bill was the kind of guy who did a lot of the flying himself, so a lot of the office procedure was left for me to do. He would come in at the end of the day of flying and we would go over things, the schedule and so forth, and look at what we had for the rest of the week.

"Bill was one of the hardest working men I ever knew. He flew a lot, but he had to do the paperwork for his company as well. We had the public transport commission to deal with, sending in monthly reports, so he never really stopped once he stepped out of the plane. You had to give him credit for the things he accomplished over the years.

"Back in those days Bill was flying in hunters as well, and he had some tent camps set up on wooden platforms back in the country. He would put a guide and a couple of hunters at a camp and check on them every few days. Bill was so familiar with the country from flying it every day that he knew where there were moose and caribou and where to put his hunters so they would have successful trips. He would bring in about thirty to fifty hunters in a season.

"The hunting then progressed into fishing. It was 1967 or 1968 that he began Michael's River in Labrador, so now he was booking fishers as well as hunters. Once I left he became involved with lodges at Sandhill River and later Wulff Lake. Bill never stopped moving ahead and was always looking to develop both his flying and outdoor businesses. As an example, it was shortly after I left that he built a hangar in Gander for his planes.

"I never knew him to have an accident. He would often be partway to a destination and have to land on a pond or lake for the night, but he knew his stuff and was an excellent pilot.

"We began to slow down a bit about 1968. Bill had all

good pilots; they all did a good job for him and we had some very good years. I left him in 1969 after ten years with the companies. It was tough for me to leave, but I had opportunities that I wanted to pursue.

"We grew up nearly next door to Bill; my family grew up with his family and we watched his kids grow up during those years from 1959 to 1969. One of the reasons I moved to Gander was the promise of having a house to live in, and that happened.

"I came up to Goose Bay in 1969 with two partners, Burt Patey and George Furey, and formed Labrador Airways, a similar operation as Bill had in Gander. In 1972 I began a fishing camp operation at Igloo Lake as an outfitter and got into it myself.

"We purchased nine Otters, five Beavers, a Cessna 185, and a small Twin Otter from Eastern Provincial Airways, and formed the Labrador airline company here.

"We flew all the materials to Flower's River for Bowater, the lumber company, and it was during the early 1970s that we were asked to operate it for them. Eventually the company bought it from them, we were flying the people in and it seemed a natural thing to do. When we sold Labrador Airways to Roger Pike in 1983 I bought the lodge for my own use.

"As time went on in the 1980s I became more involved with the outfitting myself, with Igloo Lake and Flower's River, and then on the Eagle River I had a place.

"I used to run into Bill through those years and we always maintained a great friendship although we were now in competition for booking people at our fish camps.

"I look back on the Bill Bennett days as very good days; I never had a problem with Bill. He has to be recognized for his great flying abilities and his success in business, no matter what he jumped into.

"He would buy aircraft through bids, something like eBay these days. You would place a bid on these planes and they would call to let you know if you were the high bidder. Of course, most of them were not in the best condition, you bought them 'as is' and took your chances, but it wasn't too bad if you got them cheap enough. Then you had to go and pick them up. Those aircraft were usually laid up for quite awhile and you might have to replace an engine, but even then it was worthwhile.

"The best times with him were with the aircraft business and forming Gander Aviation, then the hunting and fishing businesses he operated both on the island and in Labrador.

The Otter on floats flying over snow-covered ground.

"When I decided to leave in 1969 I offered to buy Gander Aviation but Bill didn't want to sell it. Things were slower than they had been, the charter business had been slowing and most of the big projects were finished.

"We'll never know what would have happened with both of our careers had he decided to sell it to me, but there were no hard feelings on either of our parts.

"Bill would sometimes fly off the handle for things that some of the pilots did, maybe too heavy a load or pushing the weather, and fire the pilot on the spot – then hire him back again the next day. It would be out of his system by then and forgotten.

"I always had the highest respect for Bill, for his flying ability and for his business acumen. We parted as friends and remained friends until the day he died."

Russ Smith

Russell (Russ) Smith was a guide with Bill for more than twenty years, starting in 1977, and his chief guide for most of those. He related some interesting tales of some of the adventures he had experienced during those years – some good, and some that had him worried!

Russ recounts the time Bill's private cottage, which was built on an island at the mouth of the Sandhill River, burned to the ground. The cabin was built from a log kit, had three bedrooms, kitchen, bathroom, dining room and open living room. It was a great place, with the river running on both sides, and salmon hung in pools off the island before proceeding upstream.

I had stayed in the cabin in 1985 with a party of celebrity fly fishers, and again in 1987 while filming a television show for *Fish 'n Canada*. It was a comfortable and pleasant place to base one's self while fishing the runs of salmon. Those incidents are explained in more detail later in the book in Part Five.

According to Russ, when he examined the site, it appeared that the propane tanks had not been turned off and there had been a huge explosion.

"When we went down the next morning all we saw was smoldering embers. The cabin was gone completely. When Bill came in, Harry Martin came in with him. The tanks were designed to leak off outside and not in the cabin, so I think what happened was that the tanks weren't turned off and there was a leak somewhere inside the cabin, and eventually it built up and the pilot light in the stove set off quite an explosion. Of course there's no way we'll ever know, but one of the light fixtures that was on the wall across the kitchen ended up almost in the river on the other side of where the cabin used to be, so I think it took quite a force to propel it that far. Harry figured the same thing happened.

"If Bill had stayed there that night he could have been caught up in it. I told him the cabin was only a material thing, but he was still alive."

Russ was working for Bill on the Sandhill River when Bill was leasing a cabin that had been put there by the Department of Fisheries and Oceans (DFO) in the late 1970s. The federal biologists had erected a counting fence there to count salmon passing through the river, gathering data on the river as an index of what was happening in Labrador generally. Bill leased the property at first, but later bought the facilities from them and renovated them, with the promise that they could erect the fence again when needed.

"Bill was always fixing it up anyway and making it better, even when he was just leasing it from them."

Russ would spend most of the summer at Sandhill, and later in the summer Bill would move him up to his other lodge at Michael's River. In the mid-1980s Russ was working with Bill when he began to construct a major facility at Wulff Lake. He had secured the lease for that property from a group of ex-military officers who were staying in very crude facilities at the time, and he agreed to construct a new lodge there to cater to them each year over a fixed period of time, and to other guests during the summer when they weren't using it.

"It was only Bill Bennett who would take it on," said Russ.

Russ helped build the new facility, but never guided there. "Bill had a ship come into Table Bay and drop off all the materials that came with the pre-fabricated log kit. They unloaded it on our boats and we carried it ashore, and it was all flown in from there on Otters and Beavers. It took us about two weeks to get it all in there.

"He had a couple of people come in from the company in New Brunswick or wherever he bought it to put it together, then we put the roof on it with our own carpenters. I did the electrical wiring, but I don't even want to go there. Nothing was pre-drilled. Bill was meticulous; he didn't want any wires to be visible, so I had to make sure everything was hidden inside those walls. It was quite a job.

"We were flying furniture into Wulff Lake from St. Anthony in the winter and there was a vicious crosswind. The strip only ran one way down there at that time. There were only the three of us there, Bill and myself and Clifford Pritchett. We took off and the wind took the Otter and turned it nearly sideways. There was a power line running parallel to the runway, and suddenly we were heading right for it. The skipper (I always called Bill skipper) took one look and figured we weren't going to make it over them, so he flew it beneath, between the two towers holding the cables. I looked back at Clifford and he was white as a sheet!

"He made a couple of more trips, with the crowd at St. Anthony giving him a hand loading, and we waited at Wulff Lake. It got later in the day and no sign of Bill, so Clifford figured something had happened. Sure enough, Bill called in on the radio later on and said the wind had picked up and for us to sit tight for now. We learned later that he had tried taking off on the runway and got airborne, but the plane wasn't loaded properly and it wouldn't fly for him. He set it down again, this time he ran out of strip and just got the skis down in time to land it in the bog at the end of the runway. He didn't hurt the plane at all, but it had to be lightened and the weight redistributed before he could come in again, so we spent the night at Wulff Lake, just as happy to be where we were!

"There was another time when there was a guy in there from Orvis named Lou Black. He had a casting basket with him and he could cast out a full fly line. We had ten guests there then, and there was no way you could get that many people and the pilot off the water in a single Otter. They also had eighty fish with them and their baggage, but Bill decided to try it.

"He taxied out to the far end of the lake and came as hard as he could down toward the outlet near Wulff Lake. It was a hot day, too, and there was no wind, so getting some lift to get it off the water was tough. Anyway, he got closer and closer, and now he was committed, and at the very last second he got it up in the air, but he wasn't getting any altitude. He disappeared around the corner and all we could hear was the plane heading out toward the river mouth at full power. After awhile, maybe ten minutes or so, he circled back around and he was just about at the skyline but no higher. Once again he flew out of sight and that's the last we thought about it.

"The next day we were there at the lodge when the door opened and in walked Lou Black. 'What's this all about?' I asked myself. 'We just put him on the plane yesterday.'

"Lou told us that he had spent the night at Northwest Brook, which ran into the Sandhill. The plane had blown an engine and they had put it down there. He had walked up as far as the cabin on the lower part and crossed there, then walked up the trail to the lodge. When the engine blew there was oil spraying back and covering the windshield, so Bill stuck his head out of the window to see where he could put it down safely. There were rocks everywhere, even in the bog, but there was this one spot in the river that was fairly deep and had no boulders, so that's where he set it down. It was not very big, but he got the plane in there.

"Now we had to get the guests up from there and we have to get the fish boxes up and it was about a 45-minute walk one way. So we did that and had to go back for the luggage and carry that out in a second trip. It was not easy for any of us; it took about three hours to get that done, but everyone was safe and that's what counted the most.

"We figured the only way he would get the plane back out was to dismantle it and bring it out in sections, but Bill decided he was going to change the engine in there and try to fly it out. We didn't believe it at first, but sure enough, this one day, here comes Bill and Eric Crewe and Clifford Pritchett, and we began to believe him.

"We stayed on the plane for a couple of nights and in came the helicopter with the engine, so Eric and Clifford changed it over and got everything ready. Bill and I went in then, and that's when I learned he was going to try to slingshot it out of there! He said he would tie the back of the plane to a tree, get in and fire up the engine, rev it up, and when he put his hand out of the window I was to cut the rope, and that's the way it was supposed to work.

"Eric was there too, and he was a big guy, so Bill told him that he needed a couple of hundred pounds up front and he wanted him to ride with him. Eric looked at him and said, 'Bill, I've never said no to you in my life, but…no! If you want to kill yourself then go ahead, but I'm not doing it.'

"Bill asked me, too, and I told him, 'If Eric wasn't doing it, considering how long he's been with you, then I'm not going either.' That left Clifford, who weighed about 130 pounds, and he refused as well. So Bill ranted and cursed a bit, then he asked us to bring in some rocks, and he loaded about 200 pounds of rocks in the plane up front. That's when we all figured this was it; Bill was on a suicide mission.

"Anyway, he got in and revved it up, putting the power to it. You could almost see the floats lifting up off the water. Eric and I were off to the side, and poor Clifford was behind the plane, nearly getting blown over with the force of the prop. But Bill put his hand out of the window; Eric passed the signal on to Clifford, who then cut the rope. Well, we never saw anything like it. That plane literally jumped straight up into the air!

"I think even the skipper was surprised, because it looked like he was going to lose control of it for a minute, but he straightened it out and got it flying. I tell this story to people who have been pilots, some flying in Viet Nam, and they find it hard to believe, but by God that's how he got it out of there. There's no doubt that he knew his planes. That man was meant to fly."

There were other stories, too, some pretty scary. You get to experience them when you work for a man like Bill Bennett over the years that Russ was with him.

"There was one time we were heading into Cartwright for fuel, and we got to within about five miles when we hit this wall of fog. We were right down on the water. 'We're not getting into Cartwright. I guess we'd better head back to Sandhill,' said Bill. But when we turned around, the hole had closed in on us, and we had no choice but to go up through it. Now we were on top and there was not much choice; somewhere and sometime we had to go back down.

"Bill said, 'I don't like those big hills around Sandhill, I think we'd better head down the coast to Charlottetown.' Clifford was in the plane with us this time again, and he just looked at me with that funny expression on his face, like 'what am I into this time?'

"So Bill flies for awhile and says, 'I know we're out over the ocean, so we're going down through it.' We did, and sure enough we were over the ocean and didn't have much more than a 300-foot ceiling. And it was getting darker all the time. So Bill says, 'Russ, you should see a flashing red light on your side, let me know when you see it.' So I kept looking and pretty soon I spotted it. 'Yes, that's it,' said Bill, and turned toward shore.

"As soon as we got in there Bill told us it was the wrong place, and he began cursing. We ran out of water soon enough and flew into this valley. We couldn't turn; the hills were closing in on us. Bill is picking his way from hole to hole; it's getting later and later, and I didn't give two cents for the chances that we'd ever get out of this one alive. I was smoking a pipe at the time and I had filled the bowl to light it, but forgot I even had it in my hand. Bill came down over this lake, but you couldn't see much of anything; it was nearly black, and when I looked down I still had the match in my hand and the pipe clenched in my teeth.

"Bill flew along, looking out the windows and then at his compass and then at his watch. We came to the end of the lake, and I kept wondering why he didn't set it down here, but when he got to the end he looked at his compass and watch again, then put it straight up into the fog. Everything just went black. Clifford and I figured we were done now for sure. So we flew on for awhile and then he sets the nose down and we're expecting to crash at any time. Well, we came out of it on the harbour that is about a mile across, and it's raining, just pouring out of the heavens. And there in front of us is Charlottetown.

"So we land and taxi in, and no one says a word. As we coast into the dock there's some people waiting to help us land, and one of them says, 'See, I told you it was Bill Bennett; nobody else would be crazy enough to be out flying on a night like this!'

"Of course, we asked him how he had done it. There was a guy by the name of Ace Wentzell who was building a place on the Hawk River then, and this was the lake that Bill had landed on to drop off the material. Bill recognized it when he flew over it, and he knew how long it had taken him to fly in from Charlottetown to the lake, and the compass heading he had to fly to get back and forth. So that's how he got us back that night, looking at this watch to get the exact flying time and looking at this compass to fly the exact heading.

"There was another time that we left Goose Bay for Border Beacon near the Quebec border. There was an outfitter from Labrador City who had flown three hunters in there; he was flying three more in and picking up the first crowd. It was a real windy day, and he flipped the plane when he went to land in the lake. One fellow drowned; the other three made it to shore and survived. Bill had an insurance contract to salvage it and bring it out. He picked me up at Sandhill and we flew in on the Beaver to see what it was like. We flew around it several times and took some pictures, then landed on the lake. The plane was in good shape, just upside down in the water. It was tied to the shore.

The plan he had was to tow it to the strip in a boat that's there, dismantle it, take off the wings, put the engine and stuff inside, and fly out from the landing strip that was there at the site.

"We flew down again in October, and by this time it was pretty cold in Labrador. We had Eric, Dave Morris, and Clifford with us. We got into Goose Bay and got everything aboard. We had air bags and the cylinders to blow them up so we could float the plane over to where we could work on it. When we got to Border Beacon the tail section was gone under, the left wing was under water; all that was left was the fuselage. We got an airbag through it and got it up, or otherwise it would have ended up completely sunk.

"When we went back up to get it, the weather had turned really cold. Howard Mercer was alive then, and he warned me not to go up there because he had been there three weeks before and the only lakes not frozen over were the big ones. But Bill went anyway, and when we arrived, there was not much left of the plane. The weather came down hard and beat up the tail section on the rocks, so there wasn't much to salvage. The two wings were just hanging by the cables. We got caught in a vicious storm, and by the next morning we could walk on the ice. It was too bad; that plane didn't have a scratch on it when we first went in but the weather sure took care of that."

There was another time when Russ went into a small pond with Bill and his son Noel, who at the time was about nine or ten years old. As they circled the pond Russ spotted a bull and a cow near a bog, and both Russ and Bill had licenses for them, so they set the plane down on the lake and walked to where he had seen them.

"I'll go around behind, you see if you can find where they went in," said Bill.

Russ and Noel walked down the beach and saw the cow standing there, so Russ shot her. He figured that would drive the bull to where Bill was standing, so he told Noel to get down and they both hit the beach. It wasn't long before there was a shot, and sure enough the bullet whizzed by overhead. Then there were more shots, and then a brief silence.

"How many bullets does he have?"

"I think he has nine," said Noel.

"Then keep your head down, he must be reloading." Sure enough, three more shots rang out, then nothing.

When Russ and Noel walked to where Bill had been shooting, his only response was, "I guess I missed him!"

Russ picked up the track and followed it for awhile, but the bull was running at full tilt and there was no sign of blood. When he returned to Bill's position he told Bill that he had downed the cow, and Bill's reaction was "How come you didn't shoot the two of them?"

"Bill pulled his Cessna down the beach and I was building a tripod to hang the quarters there, and he asked what I was doing, so I told him. He said, 'I figured we could take this one out now.' It was a very hot day and no wind, so I had my doubts.

"This was a good-sized moose, and all we had was that Cessna with the three of us, but he took down the rear seats and jammed the four quarters in the back, then somehow squeezed Noel in on top of the moose. 'You'll be all right there, Noel, just hang on.'

"Well, the two of us squeezed into the front and taxied it way down the lake, turned, then he put the power to it. We were heading for that bog, but I had a leg half in my face and couldn't see much out the front. What I did get a glimpse of was that bog getting closer and us not off the water. At the last minute I felt it lift off the water, but I also felt three distinct taps as the floats touched some of the brush on that bog! Anyway, we got back with the moose and Noel in the back without any more problems.

"One thing about the skipper, he knew his planes and what he was doing with them.

"Bill hardly ever logged all the hours he flew. Nobody will ever know how many hours he had in the air, especially in Labrador. Bill worked hard and never ever complained. If someone gave him a crust of bread for breakfast, he would simply say, 'Thanks, cook.' He would never ask if there was more. If he had to sleep under a boat on a bed of boughs he would never complain. He worked hard and deserved what he got for it.

"Bill had another side, too. One time he dressed up like a woman with a wig and a long dress on and had everyone fooled. He was introduced as 'Bill's sister,' and he was out on the floor dancing with some of the boys and having a great time. He could let his hair down and just enjoy having fun with the rest of us, forgetting for a short while about the flying and the lodges and all the other things he had on his mind.

"I don't think there was anything he couldn't take on or try. There were four of us that dug out the basement at Michael's River, an unbelievable job to even attempt, and only Bill Bennett would attempt it. We did it all by hand, just the four of us, bringing sand up from the beach in a wheelbarrow and probably moving tons of beach rocks to add to the concrete. It was a major undertaking, but we did it for Bill.

"You know, I always told Bill how much I hated funerals, and I found out when he died that he had me on the list as a pallbearer. I figured he did it on purpose! But Cathy phoned me and asked if I could do it, and I did – for him. It was the only time I ever carried somebody, and it's the last."

HAROLD PENNEY

Harold Penney was a long-time friend of Bill and has been on some interesting adventures with him.

One of the stories he tells is about the trip they made to Alaska to pick up two De Havilland Otters. One was dismantled in Alaska and shipped to Vancouver, BC, in a large transport trailer, while their plan was for the other to be flown back across the continent to Newfoundland.

The Otter to be flown back was located at Elmendorf Air Force Base near Anchorage, the largest US Air Force facility in Alaska. At that time they had to fly into Seattle, Washington, and then pick up a flight into Alaska from there.

"When we arrived and looked at the plane we found that it needed a lot of work. There were no instruments in the dash, they'd all been removed, there were no floats, and the engine was shot and had to be replaced. We decided we needed our engineer so Bill sent for Morris Power to come up. Bill located an engine in the States and had it shipped into Seattle, then he had to go down there to get it and then ship it up to us at Anchorage.

"The plane was really a mess when we got to Alaska, but there was a plane like it nearby that was sitting in a bog and had been abandoned, so we took the instruments out of that one and installed them in the other one. We bought some floats, Morris installed the new engine, and over the next three weeks he made the plane completely airworthy so we could fly it back.

"We finally got it in the air and began to head back east with the old engine in the back. We couldn't get a lot of altitude, about 8,000 feet, and when we hit the Rocky Mountains we were weaving through some of the mountain passes, passing over glaciers and some real wilderness country. When

Harold Penney assists with repairs on the Otter ski.

we hit the colder air we gained more altitude and were able to navigate our way through. The scenery was beautiful but we were more concerned with having enough fuel to get us to the next stop.

"It took us seven days on the return trip. We hit some bad weather coming into Quebec and headed north to avoid it, ending up in Seven Islands for a night and a day. Once we had a window of opportunity Bill said we were going to make it into Gander on the final leg and that's what we did, landing at Deadman's Pond later that evening."

In total, the trip covered 6,200 miles and Bill's flying time in the journey was 52 hours, at the time considered to be a record journey.Once back in Gander the aircraft was completely overhauled and painted with the familiar white and orange, Gander Aviation's colours.

The aircraft was then used to move helicopter fuel along the proposed transmission line that was a part of the Lower Churchill Falls Trans-Labrador power development. Bill also had two Beavers doing some of the work.

Bill and Harold met in the early days when Harold was with the Newfoundland Telephone Company. The only way in and out of the remote communities was by aircraft, and Bill had the contract to deliver the installers. Harold was one of them.

"I first met Bill in 1957. We had rented some cars from his company in Gander and were doing a lot of work on the island. We had an accident with one of them and I brought it back to Gander. Vince Burton was in the office then, and I told him about the accident and said we had lots of insurance, so no problem, go ahead and fix it. Then Bill got the news and he came out, sputtering and livid, not very happy about it. When I told him we had a lot of work and would be renting a lot of his cars he calmed right down."

There was one incident that Harold related about Bill's common sense and his knowledge of the island, and how he located them once when they got caught by weather.

"I was flying with Eddie Williams, one of Bill's pilots, and we were heading across the country toward the south coast in the Beaver. We had just switched microphones with a Beaver heading to Labrador, and Eddie thought there would be no problem because it was a short trip and he was familiar with the country, so we got off the water and into the air. In the back seat we had two girls who were on a holiday and they were just going for a ride with us. Not far out of Gander we lost power, and Eddie figured he would have to put it down in a bog, but I spotted a small lake in the distance and we were able to make it there. Of course, we had no microphone and couldn't contact anyone outside. We could listen on the radio, but there was no way we could speak to anyone.

"There was an old cabin on the lake so we got in there and built a fire and tried to figure out what to do next. I tried to fix the mike but couldn't get it to work. All we could do was listen to the radio and sit tight. When Bill found out we were overdue, he was speaking to ground search and rescue; we could hear them but were helpless to do anything. Then I thought about Morse code. I knew it, and figured someone on the rescue team might know it too, so I rigged up a transmitter from a pocket knife on the mike and started to send out an SOS – three dots, three dashes, and three dots. Bill recognized it and came on the radio.

"'Is this the plane? If it is, send me one dot.' I did.

"'Is everyone all right? If so, send me two dots.' I did that.

"There was a moment of silence, and then Bill asked, 'Do you know where you're at? If yes, send me three dots.'

"I did, and he then asked me to get out the map and let him know how far from Medonnegonix Lake we were by the number of dots, one per mile. I figured it was about sixteen, so I let him know.

"Bill drew a circle on the map about sixteen miles from Medonnegonix Lake and then asked me to let him know when he mentioned the name of the lake. He started naming them, and when he came to Newton Lake I sent him the signal.

"'Confirm that you are located at Newton Lake, fogged in, everyone is all right,' he came back to me.

"I sent him the signal and he told me the weather was down right now, but to sit tight and he would be in to get us as soon as it broke.

"We got out okay and they recovered the plane later. Of course, we took some ribbing from the boys about having the girls in there with us overnight, but I can tell you that Bill and the rescue team were up all night, and so were we. All we had on our minds was getting out of there!

"I think this was just one example of Bill's common sense approach to bush flying and knowing the country. He was one smart man.

"Bill and I became good friends over the years," said Harold. "Through the good times and the bad, the ups and downs, we always remained close friends and we shared some wonderful adventures during his lifetime. Bill was one of the pioneers that helped in the development of the province as roads were built and communications were established. The only way to get into a lot of the communities was by boat or by air, and there were times of the year when boats were useless. That didn't stop Bill. He would land a plane on skis or on floats or on wheels, whatever was clear at the time, to deliver passengers and freight and the mail to places like Fogo, Change Islands, Twillingate, or to the south coast communities like Ramea and Burgeo, Milltown, Belloram and Hermitage.

"Bill used to say that in the early days, when the plane landed, there would always be a crowd of people who came down to see who or what had landed and what he was carrying. After awhile it got to be just another plane landing, the people lost interest, even the kids didn't come down to see the plane anymore. Times were changing with the new roads and improved communications and television. A bush plane was just a novelty after those things happened. It was the end of an era.

"Bill's planes began to be used to fly in building materials and fuel for developments like the Baie d'Espoir power project near Milltown, and road construction in remote towns. Back in the mid-1970s to the mid-1980s, he had the contract to provide air ambulance service along the Labrador coast from St. Anthony up to Cartwright. He had another plane for that contract, a Turbo Beaver, which was more powerful and faster than the regular radial-engine Beavers.

"Bill would do a lot of his own flying. He loved being in the air. It didn't make much difference to him if weather was coming in. If he thought he could make it to his destination he would take off and try it. Most of the time he got through. I think he knew the capacity of his planes, and his knowledge of the country he was flying over was so great that he could set it down safely if it got so bad he couldn't fly in it.

"I know over the years Bill had a couple of engine failures to deal with while he was in the air, but to my memory there was never a serious incident while he was piloting."

Log Books

Harold and the log books that Bill left recall that it was in 1959 that Bill Bennett took his first solo flights that would lead to a career in bush pilot aviation that helped bring Newfoundland and Labrador into the twentieth century.

On May 26 he was being monitored in flight training at the Moncton Flying School according to one of his earliest log books.

Bill took his first solo flight behind the controls on June 3, 1959. He soloed again on June 5 and June 6, and the last entry in that book was June 11, 1959. At that time he had accumulated a total of only 6.7 hours.

Another log book shows entries for Bill in 1973. According to the information contained in that book, by August 4, Bill had accumulated more than 3,700 hours of flying, most of it flying bush planes in pursuit of fish and game for his guests.

It is anyone's guess how many total hours he had flown in his career, which spanned nearly forty years.

Some say 32,000 hours were logged, but many hours were not. Being conservative and guessing he flew only 1,000 hours yearly would still put him at 40,000 hours.

"We'll never really know the total," said Harold, "but it was certainly a lot!"

Bill takes a stroll to look around the country.

PART FOUR
My Years with Bill

The First Meeting

I first met Bill Bennett when I began work with the provincial government in 1984. I had been appointed to the vacant position of Hunting & Fishing Development Officer with the Department of Development and Tourism by Minister Neil Winsor, and my office was based in Corner Brook.

At that time I was new to government and how the system worked. I was reporting to Mike Joy, who was the regional tourism officer, and shared office space with him for the first few weeks. Mike eventually applied for and was appointed to the job of Director of Tourism and moved to St. John's, so I was left pretty much on my own in the office.

Once there was space available, I moved into an end office and began to organize my travel and inspection tours. My job, in part, was to inspect all of the hunting and fishing facilities in the province to ensure they met regulatory standards and to deal with some of the complaints that had been arriving at the minister's office from displeased hunters and fishers.

Another part of my duties entailed marketing and promoting the province at outdoor consumer shows in the United States and Canada and accompanying some of the writers and other media who came to the province to experience fishing and hunting. It was what some would call a "dream job," and I thrived in the position.

I would book my flying time through Newfoundland and Labrador Air Services, and attempted to spread the time around to various flying operations. Some hunting camps were so isolated they were accessible only by helicopter, and I could reach a few by a four-wheel drive vehicle, but the vast majority would be reached by bush planes on floats.

For Labrador I booked flights out of Wabush and Labrador City for western areas, in central and northern regions, I used companies based in Goose Bay, and for the coastal areas, I used the planes of Gander Aviation. This seemed to be a fair and equitable way to keep everyone happy and to spread my flying budget around to as many companies as possible.

My friendship with Bill began in that era, flying with him in central Newfoundland and along the Labrador coast.

Later, in the mid-1990s when Jack and Lorraine Cooper chose not to seek another term heading the Labrador Outfitters Association, I took over the helm and Bill joined in. He was my "right-hand," always there to attend a meeting or offer suggestions or to speak eloquently to public servants or politicians about the need to protect the industry and the fish and wildlife resources that sustained it.

There was one time when I was able to attain an audience with some politicians in St. John's who were involved in creating a way for hotel and motel operators along the Labrador coast to cater to fishing guests. Our position was that they should have to adhere to the same regulations that governed outfitting operations or that they be required to have their guests return to their facility after a day of fishing rather than staying in private cabins overnight in remote areas. We saw it as direct and unfair competition with outfitters who had invested hundreds of thousands of dollars into their operations as required by the provincial laws.

Bill Bennett and I were joined by Harvey Calden and his wife from Maine, who at the time operated a hunting and fishing camp in northern Labrador. They had flown up from Maine just for this special meeting because they were witness to what had happened in a similar situation that had occurred in Maine. They were passionate about it.

But it was Bill who expressed the most passion. He began with the conservation ethic he so strongly believed in, then got into the costs of running his business, covering the constant marketing and promotion to gain guests, the lack of reasonable salmon quota being set by the feds until just before the season began, and any number of related topics.

As he spoke, his blood pressure rose. It was readily visible. His face would turn crimson, the effect heightened by the white of his hair, and his voice would rise as he spoke, sometimes with specks of saliva showing at the corners of his lips. At times I feared he would explode, and often I had to interrupt to calm him down.

"Hey, Bill, watch your blood pressure!"

I would smile as I said it, but it always seemed to have a calming effect.

We had been given an hour to make our position known to the politicians, and I asked Bill to go first to express his thoughts. It was nearly fifty minutes later when he was finally interrupted by Beaton Tulk, the MHA for Gander, who kept looking at his wristwatch.

"Bill, I think we get your points, but the other two may want to say something as well."

Bill stopped, apologized for taking so much time, but the words he spoke came from his heart and everyone was aware of that passion for the outdoors.

Harvey finally took about ten minutes to explain what had occurred in Maine and how easily it could happen here, and I got a final wrap-up to summarize what had been said.

In the long run it didn't make any difference to the government's decision; they proceeded with their plans without duly considering the effect it may have on the existing outfitters. However, there was no hiding the fact that they had the utmost respect for Bill and his opinions. No one in the province had as much experience in outfitting and bush plane flying as he, and they listened to every word with interest and attention.

The fact that nothing changed in the final decision had little to do with our presentations, I believe it was a foregone conclusion and they had just afforded us time as a courtesy. But I will bet that those who were there that day will never forget Bill's impassioned pleas for doing what was right and proper for the existing industry.

Another time, I had applied for a job with Bill during my stint with government. My first wife Virginia and I drove to Gander for an interview with him. Bill was looking for an operations manager to help with marketing and promotion, booking guests, and relieving him of some of his responsibilities in the camp operations.

It never materialized. The first thing he said was, "Of course, I can't afford to pay you what you're making with government."

The salary was considerably lower, but I countered with a proposition that he teach me to pilot a plane along with the salary. I had been in the Civil Air Patrol in the US as a boy and had done some flying then, earning my Observer Wings in Stinson and Piper aircraft. I was enthralled with flying, but had never pursued a license.

For personal reasons I didn't take the position. Later, as we worked together on various projects, I looked back and thought we would have made one hell of a team. We'll never know what could have taken place, but in contemplating the possibilities I often wonder about what might have happened with both of our lives had I taken that job.

SANDHILL RIVER

Bill Bennett was one of the real Labrador outfitting pioneers and quite a character in his own right...and he sure knew how to run a quality fishing camp. A trip to the Sandhill River and a stay at Bill's private island cottage at the mouth of the river was one of the most memorable fishing trips I've ever experienced. I was there with the *Fish 'n Canada* film crew. I remember it for the friendship with Bill that was cemented during this brief time, and some of it because of the angling itself. It happened in the summer of 1987.

It was mid-July in Labrador, the waters on the river were just about perfect, and a run of Atlantic salmon was on. Russ Smith, Bill's long-time guide, had dropped by to see how we were settling in. He had just made his way by river boat from a site downstream to our location. The three of us were fishing a long run at one end of the island and I had just released a grilse taken on a Cosseboom when Russ showed up.

One of the show hosts, Randy Jennings, had just spent a good half hour tying in a new leader material and preparing his fly fishing tackle, and now watched, intrigued, as Russ pulled the line into his fingers and examined the long leader and fly pattern.

"Nope, no good," Russ muttered, clipping off about half of the tapered nine-foot leader. "Too long."

I watched the change of expression on Randy's face as his jaw slackened. A fly tin suddenly appeared from an inner pocket, and Russ produced a scraggly black fly with a blue throat and a patch of stiff moose hair for a wing. "A Blue Charm'll work." Russ winked.

He deftly tied the fly in place, and then took two turns of leader in half-hitches behind the head. The black fly now protruded awkwardly off the end of the short, stiffened leader, resembling a broken neck in a hangman's noose.

"Have to use 'er with a hitch, n' ya don't need much line if ya wants to catch a salmon here," Russ offered in explanation. "C'mon, now, there's usually a fish lyin' by that rock."

He pulled about ten feet of line off the reel and extended Randy's rod out toward the river. The fly on the business end danced on the water's surface, a wide "vee" flowing behind it, and we watched in disbelief as it disappeared in a sudden swirl on the second pass.

"'Ere, bye, have some fun!" Russ roared over an ear-to-ear grin as he passed the rod back to a wide-eyed Randy. Out in the rapids a silver missile burst from the waters, stripping line from Randy's singing reel as it bid for freedom from the bite of the barb. So it was that my mainland companion was introduced to the technique of hitched-fly fishing for Atlantic salmon on Labrador's remote Sandhill River. As it turned out, there was no problem to catch salmon on the Sandhill once we adopted the hitching technique, and the footage turned out to be all action for Todd's big camera.

The Sandhill River flows some forty miles from the foothills of the Mealy Mountains in eastern Labrador, fed by icy snowmelt which peaks in mid-June and keeps the waters chilly throughout the summer. It empties into the Atlantic Ocean on the Labrador coast near Table Bay, to the south of the major coastal fishing community of Cartwright.

The water is crystal clear and unpolluted, and it was on the lower stretches just in from the salt water where Bill decided to place his camps. He worked on the premise that salmon fresh from the sea are lively to hook on a fly rod, and accept a fly more readily than fish which have been in the fresh water for a number of weeks.

Over the next four days until our departure we learned a great deal about the Sandhill River. The lower reaches below the cabin were very productive for both our party and other anglers who were guests at Bill's salmon lodge above us. A series of rocky shelves extended across the river and created holding pools, or places where the salmon would hesitate momentarily on their upstream travel. The areas adjacent to our island were also excellent pools, especially edges of the rapids and near rocks which protruded from the river.

It didn't seem to matter at what time of the day we fished, the salmon would be there, rising madly for the bubbly wake which followed our "hitched" flies across the river. The technique was amazingly simple: cast the fly into the river at about a 45-degree angle downstream, keep the line taut, and cause the fly to swim on top of the surface and leave a "vee" wake behind it. It sometimes meant stripping the line rapidly to make the fly rise to the top, and sometimes retrieving line slowly to maintain the swimming action caused by the half-hitches behind the fly's head.

Randy Jennings was admittedly not the most adept or experienced fly fisherman in the world, but was eager to learn and experiment. A pro-staffer, Randy had more experience with spinning and casting rods, and was highly proficient in catching the central Canada species of salmon which had been introduced into the Great Lakes from the west decades ago. Fishing for these battling wild Atlantic salmon on a fly rod was a new adventure!

Alf Walker, a transplanted Englishman and our other fisherman, was the traditionalist in the group, steadfastly holding to the more standard patterns and proven techniques gained from fishing rivers all over the world. It was well into the second day before he succumbed to the obvious and began "hitching" his flies on a short leader and using the esthetically less beautiful but more efficient moose hair-winged flies preferred by the Newfoundland guides. Both Randy and I good-naturedly kept on his case until he hooked into his first salmon.

Bill had joined us by now and was being not only a congenial host but also our guide for the remainder of our stay. An accident to one of the regular guides had resulted in a broken limb, and Bill had volunteered to "fill in" for his incapacitated employee who had been slated to guide us.

A veteran bush pilot and owner of Gander Aviation, Bill was almost a legend in Labrador. His shock of snow-white hair, ruddy complexion and piercing blue eyes were familiar sights in most Labrador communities where Bill had spent time during the past two and a half decades, and his sometimes gruff, no-nonsense approach to doing business had earned grudging respect from those who knew him.

His Sandhill River Lodge began operation in the late 1970s and soon proved to be one of Labrador's most prolific places to fish for Atlantic salmon. A new lodge was also constructed and began operating in 1987 at the outlet of Wulff Lake, which feeds into the Sandhill River about seven miles or so up river from the sea. That lodge provided ready access to mid and upper reaches of the Lower Sandhill which were previously too hard to reach for most guests. At the new camp it was simply a matter of walking out the door and fishing the outlet pool!

Bill proved to be an amiable companion when he finally got to relax a little with us for a few days, escaping from the hectic flying and camp operating schedule which is jammed into the short Labrador summer. His knowledge of the river and feeder streams had us exploring new areas in the final hours, and a quick trip up and down the Sandhill on the last morning in a Beaver float plane added to Todd's enjoyment. With the rear door removed to help accommodate Todd's camera work, it provided a breezy but low-altitude look at the region which the TV audience could enjoy.

Our success during the four days was difficult to fathom, even in retrospect. We caught and released the daily limit of four fish easily and lost several which broke off or were not well hooked. At times it seemed that every cast brought a fish off the bottom for a look at the fly, and kept the adrenalin pumping for our trio of erstwhile anglers.

For Alf Walker, Randy Jennings, Todd Munro and me, the Sandhill River would always provide memories of some of North America's finest Atlantic salmon angling on a light fly rod, and would bring chuckles as we recalled some of the high points of the trip. Who could forget the rolling Newfoundland accent of guide Russ Smith or the first flies which Randy proudly exhibited after a half hour alone at the fly vise, or the good-natured ribbing endured by Alf as he refused to capitulate to the "hitched" Blue Charms?

We would also not soon forget the twinkling amusement in Bill's eyes as he flew a queasy Todd up and down the Sandhill River's length. Bill had promised us super fishing and he had certainly delivered the goods.

SITDOWN POND

There was once that I flew into Sitdown Pond for the first time with Bill. I'm not sure of the exact reason for the stop, but seem to recall that we were on our way to some other site and stopped in briefly to check on the place because he had experienced a few bear problems.

"Come here, I want to show you where a bear came in," Bill said.

We walked to the rear of the sprawling log lodge and he showed me a window that was about chest level to me. At the bottom of the window on the log siding were several claw marks scratched into the wood. At the side of the window were more claw marks.

"No one would believe this unless they saw it with their own eyes. That bear got his two front paws on the sides of the window and tore it out of the opening. When it fell to the ground, the window was intact, never even broke the glass. Then I guess the bear got hold of the frame and pulled himself in, with his back paws making those scratch marks below the window."

Bill opened the rear door then and we entered the kitchen. "This was a mess," Bill told me. "The bear went through the place looking for food and then left, but not through the window where he'd come in; he went out through the door."

I looked over at the door frame and could see where it had been repaired. The bear had obviously done some damage to the door and frame as it made a new hole on its way out.

The lodge that Bill had erected at Sitdown Pond is etched in my memory. It was fit for the Queen of England to stay in. It had two storeys, with suites on the top level, each with private bath, and a sprawling open living area below. The centrepiece was a floor-to-roof fireplace built from stone.

Maybe one hundred feet away was another building, a Cape Cod house that was there for the staff who would be working at the lodge. That building, in itself, was something you would never expect to find in the middle of nowhere.

All in all it was a magnificent piece of architecture constructed in the middle of the Newfoundland wilderness, inaccessible except by aircraft, or by snowmobile during the winter months. I wondered to myself how many people would never see this marvellous place due to its remoteness.

It was like all the lodges that were constructed by Bill Bennett, each a top quality facility that was a showcase for Gander Aviation's quality operations and a credit to the Newfoundland and Labrador tourism sector. In fact, it was during the week of the Newfoundland and Labrador Tourism Association's annual convention in St. John's that Bill had been spending some time at Sitdown Pond, but had to come out and fly into St. John's to accept one of the province's highest tourism awards, the Doug Wheeler Award, presented annually to one recipient who exemplifies a high quality operation in the province.

The award was named for a former employee of the Tourism Department, Doug Wheeler, who was known as "Mr. Tourism" by many because of his dedication to the sector. The late Mr. Wheeler would certainly have been proud to see Bill's name inscribed on the award that year.

I was sitting at the same table with Bill when his name was announced and he walked up to the podium to receive the honour. It was the one time I believe Bill was at a loss for words. He fumbled through some sentences, trying to express his gratitude for being recognized this way for his efforts, but I think he was really overwhelmed by the attention and recognition from the audience. I even think he may have been humbled by it all.

I do recall how proud he was when he returned to the table. It was evident in his eyes and in his face.

From my point of view he had every reason to be proud. His lodges were a benchmark for others to attain, some of the finest to be found anywhere in eastern North America, and he certainly set a standard for others to follow.

SOMETIMES A POOR MEMORY

Bill was noted for having so much on his mind at times that he forgot certain things, perfectly understandable when you are juggling the operation of four outfitting lodges and a fleet of aircraft flying in various parts of the province.

When I was first investigating a site at the head of English River where I was contemplating erecting an outfitting lodge, it was Bill who flew in my little party of four for an exploration trip of a few days. Our objective was to check out some of the places on the lake where we hadn't been so far but had seen from shore some very nice rises by some substantial looking trout.

My pilot on a few previous trips was Wes Mitchell, and Wes was the owner of a Coleman Scanoe, a 17' square-stern rig made of a very durable plastic material. Wes had agreed to fly it into the lake and leave it there for me to use, and he did – landing one fine afternoon and dropping it off on his way to the coast with a couple of fisheries officers.

I had with me one of my long-time friends, Perry Munro, and two of his friends who lived in the Annapolis Valley of Nova Scotia: Allister Lantz and Jim Wilson. We had flown into the lake with Bill on Friday in the teeth of a summer storm, landing the Beaver on the south shore of the lake and disembarking to set up tents and our gear while Bill took off

Bill and his familiar Beaver, XPC, somewhere in Labrador.

on his way to his lodge at Sandhill River before the storm reached full force.

Wes and the Scanoe arrived on Saturday, and we enjoyed fishing our way along the lake in the watercraft which was powered by two oars.

Sunday passed, and we were all packed, ready to leave, expecting Bill to arrive at any minute as previously arranged. Daylight waned and we were forced to unpack our tents and set them up again, spending the night under canvas. The boys had missed their plane back to Nova Scotia, but there was nothing we could do under the circumstances.

Monday rolled around and we stayed near the campsite, reluctant to wander too far in case Bill showed up to take us out. Weather was great, so we figured something had happened to the aircraft the previous day that prevented him from flying in. We anticipated his arrival all day, careful to stretch our declining food supply, which had been planned for a two-day stay. By day's end it was obvious we weren't getting out that day either, so the tents went back up and we snuggled down for another night.

With no form of communication we were really at the mercy of Bill's schedule. He was our transportation link and the only one who knew exactly where we were in the middle of this wilderness.

Tuesday morning we ate the last of our food, a sparse meal indeed, and took down the tents. Noon passed. Finally, in the early afternoon we heard the drone of a radial engine approaching from the west. It was an Otter painted with the colours of Gander Aviation, the orange and white standing out against the blue sky.

The plane circled and landed, taxied up to our site, and shut off the engine. To my surprise it was not Bill Bennett who climbed down from the cockpit, but Bill Smith, a pilot who flew for him from the Goose Bay float-plane base.

We learned that Bill Bennett had returned to the island on the weekend to take care of some other business there and had evidently forgotten about picking us up on Sunday evening. Bill Smith had been going over the log books on Tuesday and had not seen an entry for our return trip, so he came out to see if we were still there – luckily for us.

Later, while attending various outdoor consumer shows in the US, I heard a few others commenting on being left stranded for hours or days when Bill didn't return as had been agreed.

Obviously it could have been much worse for us if Bill Smith hadn't checked the logs, but we were never upset about the incident. I always felt that Bill figured we were self-sufficient enough to survive until he could get back to us. Bill was the type of guy I couldn't get mad at, no matter what. We would just laugh it off as "one of those things" and get on with whatever it was we were doing at the time.

If I had half as much on my mind as he did in those days, I would probably have lost track of much more!

BILL BENNETT, THE MENTOR

It was a few years after this that I decided to build a cabin at Awesome Lake, at least some sort of shelter which would be an improvement over the small tents we had stayed in previously. I contacted Bill and asked him if he would transport some lumber and plywood to the lake and drop it off where I could get at it.

The plan was to go in again that year, I believe it was 1989, to build a platform for a large wall tent that I had acquired. I was to be joined by Perry Munro and Rick Penney, two friends from Nova Scotia with whom I had fished many times in the past, as well as Perry's son Todd and my brother-in-law Herb Goldsworthy.

I had been on a fishing trip in western Labrador with Ken Schultz, fishing editor for *Field and Stream* magazine, and Ken decided to join us for a few days when that trip had ended. I used Bill's flying service in Goose Bay to transport us in, and for the first two days Ken and I worked our way around the lake in the Coleman Scanoe with a depth and fish finder, scanning the bottom for depth and seeing some huge blips show up on the screen as we passed over fish.

It was then that I decided to pursue development of the lake and river system, to build a lodge and an outfitting operation. I'd been developing business plans for the previous two years to see if it was viable, and in the end I decided to take the plunge.

It meant that I would have to leave the government job,

but by this time I was discouraged by the politics and inherent lack of consideration for the industry by the Members of the House of Assembly (MHAs), so I looked around for something else to live on while investing in the development. As luck would have it, the Atlantic Salmon Federation was seeking a Regional Coordinator for Newfoundland & Labrador, Prince Edward Island and Nova Scotia. I applied and got the job. Now I could resign and begin my dream of having my own lodge in the middle of Labrador.

It was Bill Bennett that I went to for advice. Who better to mentor me in the building of an outfitting business than the man who had a successful one going?

Bill and I had discussed it earlier, in fact, during an outdoor consumer show held in San Mateo, California. I had a booth there on behalf of provincial tourism, and Bill had arranged to join me to see about drumming up business there for his lodges.

He stayed in the hotel, sharing a room with me for the days of the show, and the tourism booth was a base for us to use in our promotional efforts – me to promote the province, and Bill to wander the halls with its many booths to purchase

Bill climbs aboard his Beaver at Awesome Lake, late 1980s.

tackle or speak to some of the sponsors.

I began small and built it slowly, based on Bill's wise advice, and thanks to his experience and wisdom, the lodge and outfitting operation became successful. Since mine was strictly a brook trout operation and Bill's lodges focused on Atlantic salmon and Arctic char, we agreed to cooperate in our marketing efforts. For any inquiries I had for salmon or char I would bring out Bill's brochures to promote his lodges, and he did the same for anyone seeking to fish for large brook trout.

We worked together, and I appreciated his efforts on my behalf as I'm sure he appreciated mine on his behalf. I'm not sure if either of us actually gained a booking directly from the other's efforts, but at least our brochures were in the hands of fly fishers and they were exposed to both of our operations.

A Few Other Incidents

Another time stands out in my memory. Bill and I were in St. John's to meet with Vince Burton to discuss who would be given a contract to write a proposal for government on behalf of Labrador outfitters. At that time I was president of the association.

I had made a proposal to federal fisheries for funds under the CASEC (Canada/Newfoundland Agreement for Salmon Enhancement and Conservation) agreement to conduct a study of potential for expansion of the Labrador sportfishing industry and received approval. Bill and I had developed guidelines for the study and called for proposals by advertising in the *Evening Telegram*, which got around the entire province. We had three or four proposals to consider, and studied all of them. The contract was finally awarded to Dr. David Snow, who ran a consulting company in St. John's.

We had driven out to the city in my Dodge Caravan. On the return trip, which was well after dark, we broke down on the Trans Canada Highway just before reaching Holyrood. We later learned that a wire had shorted out near the battery, but the breakdown required us to be towed back into the city for repairs. The van was left at Dodge City, so Bill and I bunked down in one of the local motels until the following day when we could get back on the road.

Bill was not upset or concerned by the delay. We had a chance to discuss the funding and how it would be administered, plus other business of the outfitters association. If not for that breakdown we may never have had the opportunity to do that. It was beneficial for both of us, helping to cement the relationship we had developed.

THE SOGGY HAT

Another time Bill was flying into St. John's and asked if he could borrow my vehicle which had been left at the airport. I gave him the keys and asked him to leave them at the desk because I would be flying in a few days later and needed the vehicle to drive home to Clarenville.

I had just acquired a new wide-brimmed felt hat, a Stetson, and had spent a fair chunk of change on it at one of the sports shows. It had a great shape and fit like a glove. I had left it lying in the back seat.

When I flew into the city a few days later the keys were at the desk as I had asked. I went out to the parking lot and found the car where Bill had left it. Unfortunately, the battery was dead. He had turned on the interior light, probably to collect his belongings, and had forgotten to turn it off.

In the back seat was my hat, but it didn't resemble anything like the way I had left it. It seems that it had been raining in St. John's when Bill arrived, and he had "borrowed" my hat to keep the rain off his head as he completed his business dealings around town.

When he returned to the vehicle he had tossed it on the rear seat and forgotten about it. Soaked, the hat had taken on a grotesque shape and had shrunk as it dried.

Later, when I was talking to him on another matter, I mentioned that he had forgotten to turn off the interior light but I had arranged a boost with someone parked near me. He apologized for that and then thanked me for the use of my hat.

"Nice hat, Len," was all he said. "I got a loan of it. A lot of rain was coming down. Hope you didn't mind."

I didn't mention the condition of the hat to Bill. That hat went with me to Labrador the following year, and I used it as a felt filter for straining gas for the outboards and generators. It probably served a more noble purpose at the camp than it would have keeping my head warm and the sun out of my eyes.

THE USED TRUCK

Bill was always buying and selling things. I think it was in his blood from his automobile days.

I was looking for a used vehicle in which to carry my booth to shows in the US, and mentioned it one day in conversation with Bill. That's when he told me that he had a used GMC Suburban parked at his warehouse down at Deadman's Cove, and he would give me a good deal on it if I was interested.

My wife Ruby's son Tony Blackmore was a good mechanic, so I talked him into coming to Gander with me to look at it. If it was something in decent shape then I would drive it back to

Clarenville and he would drive back in our other car.

Bill went to the warehouse with me to look at it and brought along a battery so we could start it. We checked the fluid levels and all seemed fine, so we cranked it over and it started without a problem. That's when I found out it was a vehicle that Bill had bought from Newfoundland and Labrador Hydro at auction, one of several he had acquired. This was the last of them.

I wanted to get it on a ramp to see the exhaust system and check for rust, so we pumped up one of the tires that was flat and I drove it up to a service station on the Trans Canada that Bill used for servicing his vehicles. We got it on the ramp and the Suburban didn't look too bad, except for the brakes, so I had the mechanic install those and check everything over for inspection so I could get it licensed. I had pretty well figured I would get it and make it work for me. I paid for the brake job and inspection, and then drove it back to Bill's office.

When I went in to discuss the Suburban, I told Bill that I had paid for the work and had a total of two thousand dollars left to buy it. That was the limit of my budget at the time. It was probably not a lot of money to Bill, but it was to me.

"I could probably get four thousand for that truck on a trade," he told me. He looked at me over the rims of the glasses perched on the end of his nose, looking pretty serious.

"Well, Bill, that's all I have to spend on the vehicle, so I guess you have to either sell it to me for that or reimburse me for the work I paid for and I'll be on my way."

I guess he figured I was not going to budge. There was about a minute of silence, and then he said, "Well, you've been a good friend to me, and you need it, so if that's all you've got, then I guess I'll have to sell it to you for that."

I pulled out my cheque book and wrote him the cheque, very

appreciative. That truck lasted me for another four or five years. I drove it to the States for shows and never had a problem with it.

That day, I drove it back to Clarenville without it being legally licensed or insured, and thankfully was never stopped by a policeman. Tony hugged my rear bumper all the way so no one could spot the sticker on the rear plate. It hadn't been licensed for a couple of years!

Later, some people said that Bill must have been in an exceptional mood that day to sell it so cheaply or that maybe he just wanted to get rid of it, but I figured it was a demonstration of our friendship and he was sincerely helping me out. It never bothered me either way; the Suburban worked out fine and was well worth the money. And yes, it really was all I had to spend.

DROPPING BY

When I moved back to Newfoundland from New Brunswick after my job with the Atlantic Salmon Federation became redundant, my second wife Ruby and I bought a small two-bedroom house in Shoal Harbour near Clarenville. The house was protected by trees and was hard to find unless you had directions. I had my office set up in one of the bedrooms.

Bill would drop in, always calling first, when he was out my way. Later, when Ruby and I bought a larger house and developed Whitehall Country Inn, he would drop by there. I remember that he came out once to speak to a boat fabricator about building some Gander River boats, but for some reason that project never got off the ground.

Whenever I was passing through Gander I would stop in to see Bill. I knew where his hangar was and had been there previously, so one day when I was in the airport town I decided to drop in unannounced to see what he was doing. It was in the winter.

I walked into the hangar and trudged up the stairs toward the section where his office was located and ran squarely into an RCMP officer who had just come out of one of the doors.

"What are you doing here?" he asked suspiciously.

"I dropped in to see Bill Bennett," I replied, wondering what the RCMP was doing here.

"He doesn't own this anymore. The RCMP bought it. You have no right to be here, you'd better leave."

It didn't take me long to exit that building! Before I left I asked where Bill was now operating, and was directed to a new office building located in another area of town.

I stopped in and Bill was there. I told him the story and it brought a smile to his face. I had no idea that he had sold the hangar and relocated, and I think he was amused by my apparent discomfort at being caught in that situation.

The last time I was in Gander and dropped by his office it was closed. I think it was after he had sold one of the Labrador lodges and things had slowed down for Bill and his businesses.

I believe it was toward the end of his flying days, and maybe he had come to the realization that he would not be able to get into the sky again behind the stick of his planes. What a sad realization that must have been for a man who had spent most of his life in the air, flying over the wilderness that existed in the early days when the province was growing and his flying services had been so vital.

"Times have changed," he told me during a telephone conversation only days before he died.

"How true," I replied. It was the last time I spoke to him.

PART SIX
OVER AND OUT

A TRIBUTE: SO LONG, BILL

(Written for the *Atlantic Salmon Journal* following his death)

A late summer storm was not unusual in this part of Labrador. Winds coming off the high peaks of the Mealy Mountains could whip the lake into froth in seconds. Storms sometimes lasted for a few days. This one lasted for three.

Looking out at the whitecaps I couldn't imagine anyone flying in this weather, yet I could swear I heard the thrumming roar of an aircraft engine over the howling wind. As it turned out, my hearing was accurate.

Moments later the familiar white and orange colours of Gander Aviation's De Havilland Beaver passed low over the lodge, tossed about by the heavy gusts, and finally set down in a protected cove on the far side of the lake, a good mile away. The aircraft then became a boat, a very cumbersome one. It took the pilot more than an hour to cautiously traverse the distance from that cove to our side of the lake. At times we swore the wind would tip it over as a wing would be raised, nearly lifting the float from the surface, but somehow the pilot held it together.

Eventually it was taxied to the only other quiet place on the lake, a sheltered beach about a quarter mile away where we kept our boats during stormy weather. I was there on the shore, ready to give a hand, when the plane finally shut down its engine and coasted to a stop on the sand.

The door popped open and down climbed my old friend, his ruddy complexion and shock of snow-white hair readily identifiable. I should have realized it would take a bush pilot with years of experience to master this situation.

It was Bill Bennett who tossed me the rope and grinned, his only comment being, "Some windy! How you doing, Len?"

Bill was a lodge guest for the next three days. He had been caught by the sudden windstorm while en route from Goose Bay to his lodge at Sandhill River. Battered by the headwinds, he was lower on fuel than expected and made for my place as a refuge and possible fuel stop. When the storm abated on the third day, Bill borrowed a drum of gas, refueled, and went on his way.

The following summer his Beaver appeared again out of nowhere one sunny afternoon, tied up to the dock, and Bill dropped off the drum of fuel he had borrowed the previous year. He was like that. He always paid his debts.

Bill and I went back nearly two decades. When I worked with Tourism we had shared a booth and a hotel room at an outdoor consumer show in San Mateo, California, flown over much of Labrador together on inspection tours, and hosted a film crew from the *Fish 'n Canada* TV show at his private camp on Sandhill River.

When I began in the outfitting industry it was Bill who flew in the first load of lumber, and over the years he was an encouraging force in the building of my young business. We cooperated in promoting each other's operations at consumer shows and worked together to promote not only ourselves, but Labrador in general.

Bill Bennett's exploits as a pioneer bush pilot and keen businessman in Newfoundland and Labrador were well known and recognized by his peers. He was also an avid conservationist who fought tirelessly for better management of salmon and trout stocks.

When I assumed presidency of the Labrador Outfitters Association, a stint that lasted three years, Bill was my right-hand man, always there to support and speak out on issues. At meeting after meeting we represented the industry, fighting for sustainable resources and a management plan which gave outfitters a predictable future.

Whether it was a Minister of the Crown or a public servant, Bill spoke the same message to both, and we achieved some success due to his position of respect and his impassioned pleas. Everyone listened to Bill. He was very persuasive.

We visited one of his old friends in Gander Bay a few years ago, a former guide named Dominic Francis, and I learned about the humorous side of Bill. While driving there he told me this story about the days before a road connected to Gander Bay and electricity served the area. Back then there was only one way to reach the several small communities and that was in a slender boat via the fifty kilometer-long Gander River.

Bill went down to Gander Bay in one of those boats from Glenwood, armed only with a photo and a set of dishes, selling gasoline-powered washing machines. He went door to door, showing the photo and explaining that the washing machine came with the dishes as a bonus.

He sold so many washers that a freight car on the old Newfoundland railway was sent out to the siding at Glenwood with a full load of washers, and it was several weeks before all the machines were picked up and carried downriver by the buyers. Wash day was never the same after that. Gander Bay echoed to the chugs of the gasoline engines. You see, I told you he was persuasive!

Bill called me out of the blue recently to see how I was doing. We chatted as old friends do, about everything under the sun and nothing in particular, updating each other on what had transpired in the past year or so since we'd crossed paths. The face of Labrador was changing, he said, and things were not the same. Less than a week later he was buried.

Death came suddenly to Bill at age 70, a shock to many, me included. It will seem strange not to see that shock of white hair, flashing blue eyes, ruddy complexion, and quick smile anymore, but the tales and exploits of Bill Bennett will live on. They are woven into the fabric of the province, in the development of Labrador, in the history of the town of Gander, and in the memories of those who flew with him or knew him.

Whether he realized it or not, Bill Bennett was a pioneer and a legend in his own time.

Newfoundland & Labrador House of Assembly

As an example of how respected Bill was, you have to consider what took place in the Newfoundland and Labrador House of Assembly shortly after Bill died. It was Sandra Kelly, the Member of the House of Assembly (MHA) for Gander, who stood and related this to her colleagues and fellow politicians.

MS. KELLY: Mr. Speaker, may I ask leave to present a member's statement on a matter from my district, a passing of a very prominent citizen?

MR. SPEAKER: Does the Hon. Member have leave?

AN HONOURABLE MEMBER: By leave.

MR. SPEAKER: By leave.

MS. KELLY: Thank you, very much.

I rise before the House today to pay tribute to the late Bill Bennett, who passed away on April 21 at the age of seventy. Mr. Bennett was a well-known bush pilot. He was well-known in Gander and Appleton, and indeed all around this Province. Many knew him through Gander Aviation, his air service and charter company which was in business for nearly forty years. He was well-known for providing air ambulance services to hundreds of communities in our Province, particularly as part of the Grenfell Mission. He provided a valuable lifesaving service to those in isolated communities who required medical attention. Mr. Bennett would often transport patients to the nearest hospital in stormy weather conditions, risking his own life to save others.

In his lifetime, he accumulated more than 30,000 hours of flying. A true pilot at heart, Mr. Bennett was still flying his one plane, a Beaver, last summer.

He was also very well-known for his hunting and fishing lodges both on the Island portion of our Province and in Labrador. His lodges attracted visitors from around the world. An expert sportsman himself, Mr. Bennett took a hands-on approach to the business and would often personally assist guests with hunting and fishing. His passing is a sad event for the District of Gander, for our aviation industry, and indeed for this Province as a whole.

Mr. Speaker, I would ask that you send a letter of condolence to the family of Mr. Bennett, on behalf of the Legislature. Thank you.

OVER AND OUT

At Bill's funeral there was an overflow crowd who came to pay their respects. During the church service, at an opportune moment when the priest was facing the altar, his daughter Cathy rose from her seat and walked to the front of the church to deliver a eulogy for her dad that she had written while a passenger on the plane from Toronto.

It was not supposed to happen. There was no place in the service where this was permitted, but Cathy, being her father's daughter, would not take "no" for an answer. She summoned the courage to ascend to the podium where a sermon would normally be given to deliver a final message for her father. It went like this:

> As we all know, we sometimes have no control over what happens in our lives. Life throws us many

curves to deal with and sort out...both good and bad, happy and sad. We are all shocked and saddened by what brought us all together today...the sudden death of our dad, Bill Bennett. No one is ever truly ready for this moment.

For the next few minutes, let's look past the sadness and grief, and into the life of that unique individual "with that shock of white hair."

Bill left his mark on all of us and most definitely on the Town of Gander and the people of Newfoundland and Labrador. From a scrawny young man, without two nickels to rub together, he founded Bennett Motors.

There's a book entitled They Had A Dream. *Both Dad and Noel are in that book... as well as a few other pilots that are here today. Dad always had a dream to fly and against all odds he pursued that dream. He sold Bennett Motors and then proceeded to get his pilot's license. He tried and failed and then tried again. With license in hand, he boarded TCA for Toronto where he bought his first airplane, a Cessna 170, got his float endorsement in Toronto Harbour, and as a new pilot, flew the Cessna from Toronto to Gander.*

He never gave up that dream!

With pilot's license in hand, he founded Gander Aviation. He was the bush pilot pioneer that relentlessly flew into the remote coastal areas providing food, mail, ambulance service and medical supplies. And then he went on to build a successful hunting and fishing operation.

"God, he worked hard!" and he taught us ALL that attribute. Dad was always building, always working, and always dreaming... and he still was up

until April 21st. He still went into the office. It was important for him to check in, to keep busy, and to have cookies with Doreen.

And, boy, anyone who has ever sat through one of Dad's stories can attest to what a "yarn" he could tell! We would all be on dessert and Dad hadn't finished his salad!

Bill Bennett had a different time zone than ours. We all grew up waiting many, many hours to go somewhere...until we finally adjusted to BST – "Bill's Standard Time!"

I think in the last few years we all feared he might leave us as a result of a flying accident, but he had the good sense to know when to "retire his wings."

His heart and soul were up in those clouds. We all know the sound of Bill's Beaver – the XPC. That was his baby...and the stories of him trying to reach air traffic control after dark to close out his flight plan... and his blasted radio not working again! He was the VFR guy landing as the IFR guy.

Dad, you were and are a legend. And it seems everyone knew you or knew of you.

We ALL bragged about you!

Dad – from Mom, Michael, Patrick, Noel, Terri, Colleen, and myself, Cathy, we love you and will miss you always.

You did it your way. Over and out!

A plaque marking Bill's passing sits high on a hill above Michael's River.

Noel Bennett carries on with his father's love of flying.

EPILOGUE

I HAVE DIFFICULTY ending this book and sending it to Bill's family for their review and approval. I feel that there is so much more that should and could be said about this man, William James Bennett, or just plain "Bill" as everyone knew him.

Bill was a singular type of man, an adventurer who took chances yet knew his limitations, a gutsy individual who built one of the province's most successful businesses and in doing so touched the lives of so many people. Previous generations probably would have referred to him as a "man's man." Bill did things that other men only dreamed about.

There are probably several hundred more stories that could be included here, events that are remembered because Bill Bennett was involved in them. I'm sure there are many who will feel they were overlooked and have their own stories that should be included. To those people I ask only that you forgive the omission and try to remember fondly the man with that shock of white hair who flew into your life and left a lasting impression.

Bill's careers in aviation and in the outfitting business are legend, and those are the events I have attempted to relate.

His personal life, you will find, is not mentioned, because that is not what this book is about. Just the fact that he had time for a personal life is a wonder.

He engendered respect from everyone who ever knew him. While many important figures would often want to be referred to as "Mister" or "Sir," that was never the case with this man. Whether it was the premier of the province or the man on the street who was filling up his vehicle at a gas station, he was always known as "Bill." He built an instant rapport with everyone.

There is a small display located at the North American Aviation Museum in Gander that recalls some of Bill Bennett's exploits during his four decades of flying in the frontier of Newfoundland and Labrador. If you haven't stopped there to visit, you should. It may help connect you to the part he played in the province's history that you weren't previously aware of.

What more can be said? I feel fortunate that I knew Bill and spent a short time in his life doing things together. He was a colleague and a friend. It is still hard to believe he is gone.

He is missed, but will always be remembered because his life and his achievements are woven into the fabric of Newfoundland and Labrador. Future generations will look back on his life and wonder how one man could have done so much in seventy short years.

Bill Bennett. There will never be another like him.

A trip downriver in a Gander River boat brought a smile to his face.

BORN AND RAISED in New York, Len Rich moved to the Corner Brook area in 1966. A prolific and award-winning writer, Len has achieved recognition from several writers' organisations. In 1991, the Governor General awarded him with the *Canada Recreational Fisheries Award*, in recognition of outdoor writing and contributions to conservation, which "influenced a generation" of sport fishers. *Bill Bennett* is his seventh book.

Other books by Len Rich include...

Memoirs of a Fly Fisher
So You Want to be An Outfitter
Rivers & Woods
Fly Fishing Tips & Tactics
Newfoundland Salmon Flies...and How to Tie Them
Best of In The Woods
Tales of Christmas (ed.)

www.ingramcontent.com/pod-product-compliance
Lightning Source LLC
LaVergne TN
LVHW021524080426
835509LV00018B/2647